Gaelic Folklore

selected by

PETER RAMAKERS

This first edition published in 2020 by
Gwasg y Dderwen

Cover image: Glencoe, Scotland

ISBN: 978-1-8383440-0-9

ACKNOWLEDGMENTS

Thanks to Teleri Lea for help with the logo design.

CONTENTS

1 *SÌTHCHEAN*, FAIRIES

Introduction

The fairies in Gaelic are called *sìth,* meaning 'peace' as referring to their silent motion. Broadly there are two categories of fairies, those of human size and small beings. As differentiating terms we may use *daoine sìth*, 'fairy people' for those of human stature and *daoine beaga*, 'small people'. A single fairy is a *sìtche*, the plural is *sìthchean.*[1]

A further classification of fairies is given by Croker and Yeats, who were among the first Irish folklorists, and is as follows:[2]

The *leprechaun* or *cluricaun*. The little shoemaker. If you can keep your eyes on him and catch him, he has to give you a bag of gold.

The *gean-canogh*, or 'love-talker.' He is like a leprechaun, but somewhat larger. He is a great idler. He always has a pipe in his mouth and spends his time in making love to shepherdesses and milkmaids.

The *fear dearg*, or 'red man.' This spirit can be dangerous, but he also acts as a helper of humans caught in fairy spells. It may apply to small fairies, as we will see examples of 'little red men' below. Red may refer to their coats or hats, or a reddish skin colour, or perhaps to red hair. When it concerns the human sized fairy, it refers to his red hair.

[1] Campbell, J. G. & Black, R. (ed.), *The Gaelic Otherworld* (Edinburgh: Birlinn, 2008), p. 4.

[2] Croker, T. C., *Fairy Legends and Traditions of the South of Ireland*, vols. 1-3 (London: John Murray, 1825 and 1828) and Yeats, W. B., *Irish Fairy Tales* (London: T. Fisher Unwin, 1892), pp. 227-8.

The *bean sìth*, or banshee or 'fairy woman.' A female spirit of human stature who announces by wailing the death of members of old families.

A further useful classification is given by one of Evans Wentz's informants, whom he calls 'Mrs. X', who stated: 'Among the usually invisible races which I have seen in Ireland, I distinguish five classes. 1) There are the Gnomes, who are earth-spirits, and who seem to be a sorrowful race. I once saw some of them distinctly on the side of Ben Bulbin. They had rather round heads and dark thick-set bodies, and in stature were about two and one-half feet. 2) The Leprecauns are different, being full of mischief, though they, too, are small. I followed a leprecaun from the town of Wicklow out to the *Carraig Sidhe*, 'Rock of the Fairies,' a distance of half a mile or more, where he disappeared. He had a very merry face, and beckoned to me with his finger. 3) A third class are the Little People, who, unlike the Gnomes and Leprechauns, are quite good-looking; and they are very small. 4) The Good People are tall beautiful beings, as tall as ourselves, to judge by those I saw at the *rath* in Rosses Point. They direct the magnetic currents of the earth. 5) The Gods are really the Tuatha De Danann, and they are much taller than our race. There may be many other classes of invisible beings which I do not know.'[3]

This classification clears up something which is somewhat confusing in the stories. There little fairies are sometimes described as looking much like humans and being very beautiful, at other times they are described as more gnome-like. So it appears they are two distinct classes.

[3] Evans Wentz, W. Y., *The Fairy-Faith in Celtic Countries* (London: Oxford University Press, 1911).

The 'little red men' could belong to the gnome or leprechaun class, or they may be a class of themselves.

Then there is the *glaistig*, an old woman who is the guardian of the mountain deer, but who may also help on farms as the household spirit.

The *each uisge*, or 'water horse' or kelpie, is a treacherous horse that appears near rivers and lakes. It tempts the wanderer to ride it, but then gallops off and disappears beneath the water, rider and all.

The *uruisg* is a mischievous spirit living near water.[4]

Now that we have surveyed the main classes of fairies, let us turn to a selection of stories from Scotland and Ireland that exemplify their traits and habits.

Peter Ramakers
Llanfrothen, Winter 2020

[4] Throughout this work I have retained the spellings of the individual authors, who sometimes used a phonetic spelling. So you will find *urisk* for *uruisg*, *glastig* for *glaistig* etc.

Torr-a-Bhuilg

Long ago a poor woman happened to call in a house near Torr-a-Bhuilg. At the time there was no one in the house but the housewife and what appeared to be a little child. The child kept tumbling about on the floor and screaming incessantly day and night.

The poor woman asked what lad she had there on the floor. The housewife answered that she did not know. 'Well,' said the poor woman, 'I know well what he is and if you take my advice you will get rid of him; but, if not, you will get enough of him.' The housewife said that she would take her advice, and the poor woman then told her what she was to do with him.

After the poor woman left, the housewife went out and brought in a basket of eggs, which she placed in a circle on the floor. While she was thus engaged, the lad kept looking sullenly at her, and said at length, roughly: 'What are you doing in that manner?' 'I am making a brewing caldron,' was the reply. 'A brewing caldron? I am more than three hundred years old and I never yet saw a brewing caldron like that!'

The housewife had no longer any doubt of the child being a fairy, but she went about her business for a while in her usual way. Then she looked out at the window and assumed a scared look and began to start back as if she beheld something dreadful. The squaller on the floor, looking askance at her for a while, at last asked what it was she beheld. 'I see,' said she, 'Torr-a-Bhuilg on fire.' He waited where he was no longer, but sprung out at the door, saying: 'My hammers and my anvil and my bellows,' and after that he was never seen again. MacDougall, *Folk Tales and Fairy Lore in Gaelic and English*

The Glengarry Fairy

There once lived in Glengarry a widow with a young child who was a boy. One day she went to the well for water; and when she was returning to the house, she heard the child, whom she had left sleeping quietly in the cradle, screaming as if he were in great pain. She hastened in, and gave him a drink as quickly as she could. This quieted him for a little while, but he soon broke out again as badly as ever. She gave him another drink; and while he was at her breast she looked at him and saw that he had two teeth in his mouth, each more than an inch long, and that his face was as old and withered as any face she had ever seen. She said to herself: 'Now I am undone, but I will keep quiet until I see what will come of this.'

Next day she lifted the lad in her arms, put a shawl about him, and went away as though she was going to the next farm with him. A big burn ran across her path, and when she was going over the ford, the creature put his head out of the shawl and said: 'Many a big fold have I seen on the banks of this stream!' The woman did not wait to hear more of his history, but threw him into a deep pool below the ford, where he lay for a while, tumbling about and reviling her, and saying if he had known beforehand the trick she was going to play him, he would have shown her another. She then heard a sound like that of a flock of birds flying about her, but saw nothing until she looked at her feet, and there beheld her own child with his bones as bare as the tongs. She took him home with her, and he got gradually better, and was at last as healthy as any other child. *MacDougall*

Two Fairy Arrow Stories

The two following tales were got from an old man of the Clan Livington, who was fourscore and five years of age at the time of relating them.

He said that his great grandfather was a small farmer on the farm of Droman in the last century (the 18th). Like the other farmers of that period, he had a small flock of sheep pasturing on the hill in the day time. But when night came he used to drive them into the sheep-pen in the byre-end of the house.

One night, his son, who was then a young lad, happened to go to the outer door to see what appearance the sky presented, before he should go to bed. He stood for a time between the two posts of the door, looking about him, when he heard, passing him with a rush, a sound like the whizzing of a flock of birds on the wing. At the same time he felt something falling behind him in the sheep-pen. Without a moment's delay he returned into the house, and found the white-faced wether dead in the pen. The wether was skinned; but on his carcase no wound or bruise, which could be the cause of death, was seen.

Not another syllable was said about the death of the white-faced wether, until the tailor of the district came to the farmer's house to make clothes. The first night after his arrival, he said to the farmer's son: 'Do you remember the white-faced wether's death?' The farmer's son answered that he did. 'Well,' said the tailor, 'it was I who killed him, and it is you who may be thankful to me for doing so.' 'Thankful to you for killing the white-faced wether! How is that?' 'Which would you prefer being killed, yourself or the white-faced wether?' 'The white-faced wether, undoubtedly. But tell me, I pray you, what you mean.' The tailor did that in a few words. He said he was under the influence of the fairies of the Carlin Fairy-Knoll, and that they took him with them on long journeys through the air in the night-time. They could not hurt any human being except by means of another; and for that reason they used to take him with them, and make him throw the fairy arrows at the person to whom they bore ill-will. 'They have a grudge,' said he, 'at you, and when you heard us pass Droman with a rushing sound, they told me to take a fairy arrow and cast it at you. I was compelled to do what they told me; but instead of aiming at you, I aimed at the white-faced wether. Fortunately for me they saw not who fell; for before the arrow reached the wether, we were a great distance away from Droman on our way to a great meeting which the fairies held at Knock in Morven. Perhaps you do not believe my story, but I will give you a sure proof that I am telling the truth. Look in the sheep-pen and you will find the arrow there still.'

The farmer's son looked, and, as the tailor said, found the arrow lying beneath the litter on the floor of the pen. The fairy arrow would kill without leaving behind it any visible wound.

The relater of the last story was herding in his boyhood near the town of Strathavon in the South country. On a clear summer day he happened to be sitting on a mossy bank, and the cattle quietly pasturing in front of him. To pass the time he began to cut a dial in the green sward between his feet. In the midst of this work he thought he heard first a humming in the air, and an instant after that, a whizzing between his feet. He turned his eye quickly in the direction whence the whizzing had come, and what did he behold but a fairy-arrow stuck in the very middle of the dial. It was at first red-hot, but in a short time the cold moss quenched it. He then put it in his pocket, and when his engagement was out, he took it home with him to Gaeldom, and showed it to his father. 'My dear boy,' said his father, 'it was thy friend who threw it, otherwise thou wouldst not have been here this day.' Then his father told him the tale preceding this, and how the tailor aimed at the white wether instead of his neighbour, who was standing in the door. *MacDougall*

The Fairies of Corrie Chaorachain

Many years ago Donald Post carried letters between Ballachulish and Fort William. A part of the road he had to travel was pretty lonely and uncanny, and it had the name of being full of fairies and other bogles. On a Hallow-e'en, Donald, after getting his business over, was returning to Corrie Chaorachain where he was staying. A good while before he reached the house, what did he see before him but a dozen fairies dancing and leaping hither and thither across the road. As soon as they noticed him coming, one of them, a slender, red-haired fairy, cried: 'We will take Donald Post with us.' But another, a fine fellow, replied: 'We will not take Donald Post with us, for he is the poor post of our own farm.' Donald then happened to look up the hill above him, and what did he behold on the green plain on the summit but a large troop of fairies wheeling and dancing like the merri-dancers. The troop on the high road also noticed them, and instantly one of them cried: 'Let us leave this,' and in the twinkling of an eye they were on the summit of the hill with the other troop. Donald did not wait to see the end of the merry-making, but kept on his way and got home in safety. After that night he never saw the fairies; but on certain evenings of the year he used to hear the murmur of their voices in the place where he had once beheld them.
MacDougall

The Rannoch Farmer's Son and the Fairies

There once lived in Rannoch a farmer's son, who fell into ill health, and who used to go to the hill, morning and evening, to see if he would get better. When summer came, and the cattle were driven to the hill pasture, he followed, and remained in charge of them until they returned home to the strath in the beginning of harvest.

On a calm, misty day he went away to gather them to the milking fold, but strayed in the mist, and was a good long time seeking them before he happened to come upon them. He found them at last grazing in a fine large corrie with green juicy grass up to their eyes. The day was warm, and a misty, drizzling rain falling, and the grass was springing up rapidly from the ground. As he was tired with the heat and travelling on the hill, he sat down on a green hillock to take a rest.

He was not long there when he heard a voice coming from the root of every blade of grass in the corrie. He looked to see if he could find out from whom the voices came, but no man, small or tall, was visible. He listened again, and when he heard the same din the third time he understood that it came from the fairies, and so he cried as loud as themselves: 'And some of it for me also!' Immediately the din of voices ceased, and then he drove the cattle to the fold.

The milk-maids were awaiting their coming, and wondering what had kept them so long. They began to milk, but before they had gone over the half, every vessel in the fold was overflowing with milk. They could not comprehend how the milk became so abundant in so short a time; at length they began to praise the weather and say it was the cause of the abundance.

The farmer's son listened patiently to all that he heard; but he said to himself that the milk was not so plentiful on every farm as it was on theirs that day, and that it would not be so plentiful on theirs either, had he left the fairies alone when they were drawing it to themselves in the corrie. *MacDougall*

Angus Mór of Tomnahurich and the Fairies

Angus Mór was a shepherd on a farm near Tomnahurich, in Inverness. On a wet, misty evening, as he was returning from compassing the hill, he thought he heard, coming out of a rock beside the path on which he was travelling, a voice like that of a young maiden whom he was going to marry that very night. He stood and listened, expecting to hear the same voice again. He heard the voice, but saw no appearance of the woman, or of a place in the face of the rock, where she could be in hiding. Thinking, then, it was echo's voice he had heard, he held on his way until he went round a point of the rock. Before him was a pretty green knoll; and as soon as he came in sight of it, he beheld the door open, and issuing thence a light like the light of day in brightness, and he heard the sweetest music that has been or will be, and the sound of dancing within. He crept towards the door, thrust his dirk into the side post, and peeped into the Fairy Knoll. It was there that the sight was. Fairy men and women, in a circle in the middle of the floor, wheeling and dancing with mad energy. But not a bit of the maiden was to be seen. He stood where he was, until a fairy came forth, and went to a brook, a short distance off.

When she was returning he went to meet her, and stood in the path before her. 'Let me pass, Angus Mór,' said she. 'No,' replied Angus, 'until thou tell me who the woman was whom I heard calling before I came in sight of the Fairy Knoll?' 'I'll not tell thee that; I may not,' said she. 'If thou do not, thou shalt not get leave to pass,' said he. 'If not with thy good will, I will in spite of thee,' said she; and she shot past him like lightning. Angus held in his hand a crook with an iron spike in one end of it, and he threw the crook after the fairy, and struck her in the houghs. She fell to the ground, and before she had time to get up, he had hold of her between his arms, and the crook laid across her breast.

'Tell me now,' said he, 'what woman was calling in the Fairy Knoll before I came in sight of it?' 'Angus Mór,' said she, 'if thou canst tell the secret of our Queen on the Bridge of Easan Dubh a week from to-night, thy wife and son will be thine.' Angus wondered greatly at these words, but he allowed the fairy to go, and he went home, and married after his arrival.

Another evening, as he was returning from the hill, he reached the rock from which he last heard the voice. He stood still at the end of it, and listened for a while, but not a syllable did he hear. He then went forward, until he came in sight of the Fairy Knoll. On looking the way of the door, he beheld a light shining inside, but he heard not a sound of music or dancing, so he turned away; but before he had gone far on his way, he saw the fairy returning from the brook, and in passing she called to him as she had done the first night: 'Angus Mór, thy wife and son are thine, if thou canst tell the secret of our Queen on the Bridge of Easan Dubh on the evening of next Friday.'

The warning, which he thus got the second time, caused Angus some anxiety, especially as he knew not what might be the outcome.

He reached the house, and his wife met him at the door. She noticed that something was troubling his mind, so she asked him the cause, and he told her everything he had seen and heard at the Fairy Knoll. 'Angus, dearest of men,' said his wife, 'let none of these things make thee anxious. We have married before the year has run out, so do not let me cause thee anxiety any longer.' 'Wife, I do not understand thee,' said Angus. Then she said: 'About a year ago a faintness came over me as I was passing the Fairy Knoll. I sat down on the Knoll, and, in a short time, fell asleep. When I awoke I was in the finest place I ever beheld, and surrounded by men and women busy dancing. I tried to go out, but whichever way I took, the fairies – for it was they – would be before me. At last one of them, who seemed to be chief over the rest, said: 'Brown-haired maiden of the laughing eyes, thou wilt get out if thou promise to be my wife, unless thou get thou chosen love in marriage before the end of the year from this night.' I was so eager to get away that I gave him my promise. But, Angus, thou wert my choice of the men of the universe; and since I have got thee before the time ran out, I am free from the promise I gave him.'

On Friday evening Angus Mór was once more returning from the hill, and when he arrived at the Bridge of Easan Dubh, he remembered it was there he was to tell the secret of the Queen of Fairies. He stood a while on the top of the Bridge, but he was not long there when he heard in the brook under him the very sweetest voice he ever listened to. He gave a peep over the parapet of the Bridge, and whom did he see cleaning and rubbing clothes on a stone in the water, but the Queen, and this was the song she was singing:

Chorus:

Thoirionn O Ró Thùraibh Thoró,
Thoirionn O is na Thùraibh Othó,
Thoirionn O Ró Thùraibh Thoró.

'S aithne dhomh 'Bheinn Mhór am Muile,
'S aithne dhomh mullach Sguirr Eige,
'S aithne dhomh 'n cat a bha 'n Ulbha,
Agus 'earball ris an teine.

Tha ceòl an talla mo ghràidh,
'S tha òr an talamh MhicAidh;
Ach tha òran an Inbhir Nis
Air nach fhaighear fios gu bràth.

'Horin O Ró Hooriv Horó,
Horin O is na Hooriv ohó,
Horin O Ró Hooriv Horó.

I know Ben More in Mull,
I know the top of Scuir Eigg.
I know the cat that was in Ulva
With its tail turned to the fire.

There is music in the hall of my dear,
There is gold in the land of Mackay;
But there is a song in Inverness
Which shall never be known.'

When she ended the song, Big Angus cried from the top of the Bridge: 'In spite of thee, woman, thou art wrong. I have now every word of thy song, and thy secret with it.' At these words the Queen started, and uttered a scream. She then lifted up her head, and when she beheld Angus on the Bridge, she said: 'Thou hast foiled me. Thy wife and thy son are now thine own.' After saying this she went out of sight, and he saw her no more. *MacDougall*

The Red-Haired Tailor of Rannoch and the Fairy

The red-haired tailor lived in Rannoch. Like the rest of his kind, he went from house to house to make clothes of the cloth which thrifty wives manufactured for their husbands and sons in bygone times.

Once as he was approaching a house, where he had a few days' work to do, evening came on, and he saw, in the dimness of the twilight, one like a very little child, running before him and keeping out of sight behind every bush and every hillock at the road side.

The tailor hardened his step, hoping to overtake the curious manikin before him, but instead of gaining, he was losing ground at every step he took. As soon as he noticed this, he began to run with all his might; but in spite of his skin, he could not shorten the distance between them. At length he lost patience so completely that he threw his big shears at the nimble little man ahead, and struck him with them in the knee joints. The fairy, for such he was, fell on his face, and before he had time to rise up, was in the tailor's arms, and the shears on his breast. 'Tell me where thou art going, my good lad,' said the tailor. 'I am on my way from the Big Fairy Knoll, to the house ahead of thee, to get a while of the breast of the wife,' replied the little imp. This was the very house to which the tailor was going. 'And what wilt thou do with the woman's own child?' said he then. 'Oh, I will put him out at the back window to my people, and they will take him with them to our place,' answered the other. 'And will they send him home when thou hast enough of his mother's breast?' 'Oh, no; never!' 'That will do,' said the tailor, and he let his prisoner go.

When he returned he found the wife before him, and the changeling in the cradle, ready to burst with crying. The wife took him up, and gave him a drink, and then put him back in the cradle again. He was not long there till he began to scream and cry once more. She took him up, and gave him another drink. But to all appearance nothing would please him but to be left always on the breast. This game went on for a few days more. But when the patience of the tailor ran out, he sprang at last from the work-table, took in a creelful of peats, and put a big fire on the hearth. When the fire was in the heat of its burning, he sprang over to the cradle, took with him the changeling, and before anyone in the house could interpose, he threw him in the very middle of the flames. But the little knave leaped out through the chimney, and from the house-top cried in triumph to the wife: 'I have got so much of the sap of thy breast in spite of thee,' and he departed.
MacDougall

The Kintalen Changeling

There was living in Kintalen a woman who had a male-child with neither the growth nor the bloom of other children his age. From morning to evening he would not cease one minute from crying, and he would eat far more food than was natural for the like of him.

It was harvest, and there was not a person on the farm who could draw a sickle but was out on the reaping field, except the mother of the child. She, too, would have been out were it not for fear that the nasty screaming thing would break his heart crying, if she should leave him in charge of any other person.

It happened that there was at the time a tailor in the house, making clothes. The tailor was a shrewd, observant man, and he was but a short time within until he became suspicious of the lad in the cradle. 'You,' said he to the woman, 'may go to the reaping, and I will take care of the child.'

The woman went away. But she had barely taken her feet over the threshold when the withered object she had left behind began shrieking and crying loudly and sorely. The tailor listened to him a good while, keeping his eye on him, till he was sure that he was nothing but a changeling. He now lost patience with him, and cried in a sharp, angry voice: 'Stop that music, lad, or I'll put thee on the fire.' The crying ceased for a while, but afterwards it began a second time. 'Art thou at it again, piper of the one tune?' said the tailor. 'Let me hear that music any more from thee, and I will kill thee with the dirk.' When the fairy beheld the frown on the tailor's countenance and the dirk in his hand, he took such a fright that he kept quiet a good while. The tailor was a cheerful man, and to keep from wearying he began to hum a tune. In the middle of the music the ugly elf raised a loud howl. But, if he did, he was not allowed to go on with his warble but a very short time. The tailor leaped off his work-table, went, dirk in hand, over to the cradle, and said to the fairy: 'We have enough of that music, take the right great bagpipes and give us one good tune of them, or else I'll put the dirk in thee.' The fairy sat up in the cradle, took the pipes which he had somewhere about him, and struck up the sweetest music the tailor had ever heard. The reapers heard it on the field, and instantly dropped their sickles and stood listening to the fairy music. At length they left the field, and ran in the direction whence the music came. But before they reached the house the tune had ceased; and they knew not who played it or whence it came.

When the reapers returned home in the evening, and the tailor got the mistress of the house alone, he told her everything that happened while she was at the reaping, and that her child was nothing but a changeling. He then told her to go with him to the Ardsheal side of the bay, and to throw him out in the Loch. She did as was told her, and as soon as the nasty little elf touched the water he became a big grey-haired old man, and swam to the other side of the bay. When he got his foot on dry land, he cried to her that if he had known beforehand what she was going to do he would have made her never think of doing such a thing again. She returned home and found her own child at the door before her, hale and sound. *MacDougall*

The Fairy of Corrie Osben and the Tailor

In Corrie Osben lived a shepherd's wife, whose child grew very peevish and difficult to nurse. Neither she nor her husband what was the matter with the child, or what was to be done with him, until the tailor came to make clothes of a web of home-made cloth newly come from the walking-mill. Next day after his arrival, the shepherd's wife went to the peat-moss, and left the child under his care till she should return. Shortly after she went away, what did the tailor hear behind him but the sweet music of the bag-pipes. He looked the way whence the music came, and whom did he see sitting in the bed but a little old grey-headed man with a pipe of straw in his mouth, busy playing a tune, to which the following verses are sung:

Uist Oireannainn! Uist Oireannainn!
Uist Oireannainn! Uist O thì!
'S fhada tha a' chaile gun tighinn
'S gu'm faigheadh an Cannan cìoch.
Uist Oireannainn, etc.

Hush! Oranan, Hush! Oranan,
Hush! Oranan, Hush! Oheé!
Long is the lassie of coming
To give the Cannan a wee
Hush! Oranan, etc.

He kept playing this tune until he heard the woman coming; then the music ceased, and he was again a little child.

The tailor told the woman nothing of what he had seen and heard while she was absent. Next day, when she went a second time to the peat-moss, he took an egg, emptied the shell of its contents, filled it with water, and placed it near the fire. The little old mannie's curiosity was so much excited by what he saw that he turned round and said: 'What are you going to do with that, tailor?' 'I am going to heat water to steep malt in,' said the tailor. 'Well, I am more than a hundred years old, and never till now did I see an eggshell used to heat water for steeping malt in,' said the little man, as he turned away and began again to play on his straw-pipe. He kept playing the tune of the day before until he heard the woman coming, and then he once more became a little child.

On the third day, the tailor told the woman what he had witnessed, and his opinion that the child was nothing but a fairy. 'And what am I to do with him?' asked the woman. 'Take him,' said the tailor, 'to the neighbouring ravine, and throw him over the bank into the water below.' The woman did as she was told, but no sooner had the child touched the water than he became a little grey manikin. He then rose to his feet in a great rage, and scrambled up the steep side of the ravine, threatening the woman with vengeance if he overtook her. But she took to her heels as fast as she could, and never looked behind her until she arrived at the house, where she found her own child laid at the door before her. *MacDougall*

Released from Faeryland

Not so long ago, a woman and her infant son, living at Rahoy, in the Morven district of Argyll, were translated mysteriously to Ben Iadain, a hill in the neighbourhood reputed to have been the domicile of faeries. As the woman herself afterwards explained, they were taken to the Black Door, that being the name then given to the faeries' main entrance to the interior of the hill. Within the hill they encountered a vast throng of people of all ages, among whom was a young lad who approached the woman and bade her not to refuse such food as the faeries might offer her, but to take it and conceal it in her clothing. He explained to her that he and his mother had been carried hither in like manner, and that neither of them could get away because of his mother's indescretion in having partaken of the faeries' food, and her bidding him to do likewise.

When the faery-in-chief learnt that the woman refused to consume any of the food supplied to her, he sent a band of his henchmen to bring in a certain man's cow. But they returned without the cow, explaining that they could not touch it, since its right knee was resting on the plant known as the dirk grass. He then sent them forth for another cow; but they came back with the news that the milk-maid on her own confession, had just put an iron shackle on it. A third time the faery henchmen sallied forth for yet another cow; but they learnt to their dismay that this cow had just consumed a quantity of the magical plant called the *mothan*.

That night the woman's husband had a dream, in which the whereabouts of his wife and child were revealed, and in which he was instructed to tie three knots in the silk kerchief his wife wore at her marriage, and take it to the Black Door. Thus equipped, the husband entered the interior of Ben Iadain, and rescued his wife and infant son.

As for the lad, who had warned the woman not to consume any of the food offered her by her captors, he still may be held captive by the faeries, for all we know! MacGregor, *The Peat-Fire Flame*

The Faeries of Pennygown

For generations people having irksome tasks relied on the help of the Pennygown faeries. Of nights they left by the hillock all sorts of jobs for them to execute – material for spinning and weaving, household utensils to repair, and the like. When they returned to the hillock in the morning, they always found the work done to their satisfaction.

But one night a cantankerous villager left by the hillock a fragment of wood he had picked up on the shore, together with instructions for the faeries that they should make out of it a tall mast for a ship he contemplated building.

'Short life and ill luck attend the fellow who asked us to do this!' said the faeries, when they examined the fragment of drift-wood, and read the instructions accompanying it.

So displeased were the faeries that the villagers, when they came to the green hillock in the morning, found none of their tasks executed, as heretofore. And never thereafter did the faeries bestow their beneficence on the villagers of Penny gown. *MacGregor*

The Faeries of the Seely Howe

When the Laird of Blelack was making preparations to leave home for the Jacobite Wars, he engaged the services of a certain John Farquharson to rid his property of the faeries inhabiting that part of it known as the Seely Howe. Although Farquharson possessed occult powers, and had won a reputation for his having dislodged faeries on previous occasions, he found it impossible to rid Seely Howe until he had provided its occupants with alternative accomodation. So, he settled them in the Hill o' Fare, near Banchory.

But the faeries took so ill to their new environment that at length they felt constrained to pronounce two curses – one upon Farquharson, and the other on the Laird of Blelack. The curse on the former ran:

'While corne and girss grow the air,
John Farquharson and his seed shall thrive nae mair.'

On the Laird they pronounced the following malediction:

'Dool, dool to Blelack,
And dool to Blelack's heir,
For driving us from the Seely Howe
To the cauld Hill o' Fare.'

Thereafter, it is said, ill-luck pursued both Farquharson and the Laird of Blelack. *MacGregor*

How the Faeries Persecuted Luran

A little distance above Ardnamurchan shore, just by the northern end of the Sound of Mull, there is a prominent hillock known as the Charmed Knowe. Here, upon a time, lived a tenant-farmer named Luran, Son of the Dark Man. Owing to some mysterious agency, every morning Luran found one of his cows dead. His suspicions were immediately directed toward the occupants of the Culver – the name given to a *brugh* forming part of the Charmed Knowe, and said to be the abode of the Faery Folk. So Luran decided to keep an eye on his cows for a night or two, in the hope of solving the mystery of their dying. During his first vigil, he saw the Culver open, and a band of faery folk stream forth from it to encompass one of his cows. Forthwith the cow was herded into the Culver; and, according to the Gaelic rendering of this tale, no one was more active at the herding of the cow than was Luran himself. The cow was killed and skinned right duly. Sewn up in the cow's hide was an elfin tailor who, while seated on the top of the *brugh*, plying his needle as a mortal, was seized by the faeries.

That night the faery festivities were inaugurated when the cow-hide and its elfin content were taken to the door of the Culver, and rolled down the slope in front of it. Luran again took part in this operation, endeavouring by so doing to show the Faery Folk that he neither suspected them for the loss of his cows, nor desired them any ill will.

On the faeries' dining-table stood many precious goblets. These Luran eyed covetously. When he imagined that none of the inhabitants of the Culver was watching him, he stole a glittering goblet, since he regarded his possession of it to be meet compensation for all his dead cows. But the faeries observed his theft; and they lost no time in pursuing him.

'Not so swift would be Luran,
But for the hardness of his bread,'

the faeries were heard to say one to another during the pursuit. As Luran was on the point of being overtaken, he heard a propitious voice, saying:

'Luran, Son of the Black One,
Get thee among the black stones by the shore.'

So Luran made for the shore, and found his way to safety by scrambling home among the rocks below high-tide mark, since neither ghost nor elf can penetrate seaward beyond the contour reached by the highest tide. And, when scrambling home, Luran could hear the cries of a person whom the faeries appeared to be beating, and whom he believed to be the very one who had advised him to make for the black stones below high-tide mark. In the morning there was found at the base of the Culver a dead cow, in the right shoulder of which was discovered a needle, just as Luran had predicted to those who told him of its situation.

The faeries' persecution of Luran was not yet at an end, however. While he was on his way to Inveraray by boat some time later, carrying with him the faery cup he had taken from the Culver, he was spirited away by some mysterious power. And that was the last that human eye ever saw of Luran and his cup.

The folk-lore of Tiree describes Luran's encounter with the faeries somewhat differently. Luran entered a *brugh*, wherein he found the faeries all asleep. On the fire was a large copper kettle, which he sought to carry away with him. In so doing, the kettle accidentally banged against the doorway of the *brugh*; and the noise it made woke the faeries, sixteen of whom now set out in pursuit of him. 'Make for the black stones on the shore,' Luran heard someone say. So, he straightway made for the shore, and escaped with the faery kettle. *MacGregor*

A Faery Tale of Sandray

The wife of a herd on the Island of Sandray, in the Outer Hebrides, made friends with a Woman of Peace, who came to borrow her kettle. This Banshee, or Woman of Peace, lived in a faery knoll not far off; and she would be seeking the kettle every day. Not a word did she utter when she came to borrow the kettle. It was her wont to enter the house silently, and appropriate the utensil without any explanation or ado. As she was in the act of quitting the house, the herd's wife would be saying to her:

'A smith is able to make
Cold iron hot with coal;
The due of the kettle is bones,
And to bring it back again whole.'

Under the spell of this rhyme, the kettle was sure to return to its owner before daybreak.

Every day the Woman of Peace came back with the kettle filled with juicy bones. And, on a day that there was, the herd's wife, before leaving for Castlebay on an errand, instructed her goodman to tell the Banshee, should she come for the kettle in her absence, whither she had gone.

'Surely it's myself that will tell her,' replied the herd. Now, he happened to be spinning a heather rope at the gable-end of his cottage when he saw the Woman of Peace approaching; and he took fear at the sight of her, fled into the house, shut the door, and refused to open it to her. Determined not to be outwitted, the Banshee climbed up to the hole that was in the roof of the house, just above the fire. Thereupon the kettle gave two jumps, and then flew out by the hole in the roof.

When the herd's wife returned from Castlebay, she asked her husband where was the kettle. And he confessed to her how he had closed the door in the face of the Woman of Peace, and how petrified with fear he was when the kettle began to jump on the hearthstone, and ultimately disappeared through the hole that was in the roof above the fire.

Night came; but with the kettle the Woman of Peace returned not. Having scolded her husband for his childish conduct, the goodwife of Sandray hastened away to the faery *brugh*, where she found the kettle awaiting her. On lifting it, she discovered it to be heavy with the remnants of the faeries' evening meal. And, as she was making off with it, she heard a voice saying:

'Silent wife, silent wife,
That came on us from the land of chase,
Thou man on the surface of the *Brugh*,
Loose the Black, and slip the Fierce.'

No distance had she travelled with the kettle before two angry dogs came bounding after her. And she thrust her hand into the kettle, and threw out to them a quarter of what it contained. But the dogs followed on; and, ere she arrived home, she had given them the entire contents of the kettle in her endeavour to pacify them.

Jealous, to be sure, were the dogs of the township of Sandray when they perceived that the herd's wife was feeding the Dogs of Peace. But never again came the Banshee to seek the kettle.
MacGregor

A Faery's Desire

Came a famishing Woman of Peace to the door of a man living on Pabbay; 'and she had the hunger of motherhood on her.' Food she was given; and there she tarried the night. Turning to her host as she was leaving on the morrow, she said: 'The desire is with me that hereafter none of the people of this Island may go in childbed.' And from that moment – so the story has it – no one dwelling on Pabbay ever died in childbed. *MacGregor*

Red Donald of the Faeries

The herd at the Spittal, above Dalnacardoch, used to see red faeries when a boy, they say; but that was in the days before General Wade built his military road through this wild countryside. On one occasion the herd was transferred by mysterious agency during the night to the house of his father, in Rannoch, several miles away. In the morning, however, despite the fact that the door and windows were bolted and snibbed, he was found dozing before the smouldering peat-fire in his own house at the Spittal. And so the members of his household surmised that he must have entered by the chimney.

And ever after that episode the herd at the Spittal was known as Red Donald of the Faeries. *MacGregor*

Dancing in Faeryland

Not very long ago (so I was assured recently in the Highlands, at any rate!), two young men were returning in the small hours from New Year festivities at Ferintosh, each of them carrying on his shoulder a small cask of whisky. They came to a spot at which they heard laughter and merriment and the strains of music, for which there appeared to be no accounting. On proceeding to investigate matters, they beheld a doorway open in a mound by the roadside, beyond which lay a large apartment brightly illumined, on the floor of which danced an inordinate number of wee people. They both entered; and one of them, impatient to be at the dancing too, hastened on to the floor without as much as depositing his cask. His companion, more suspicious of his surroundings, stuck a pin in the door-post as he entered, so as to permit of his leaving whenever he felt inclined.

Toward dawn he decided to quite the scene of merriment, taking with him his cask of whisky. But his companion, perforce, was obliged to dance on indefinitely.

A twelve-month later he returned to the scene in the hope of being able to rescue his friend. There, to be sure, he found him, completely enchanted, dancing and dancing and dancing, with the cask of whisky on his shoulder, and resentful of any suggestion that he should be escorted home until he had finished the reel then in progress.

When, eventually, his friend was able to persuade the Little Folk to release him from his enchantment, and once more brought him into the daylight, it was observed that he had danced himself away to mere sking and bone. Here was a man under faery spell, who, like Rip Van Winkle and Mary Rose, was unconscious of the lapse of time during his enchantment, since in Faeryland a year is as a day! *MacGregor*

A Host of Faeries

Mention of the cask of whisky reminds one of a glen in Balloch that long was regarded as the abode of a tribe of faeries. To this day the old folks of Loch Lomondside recite the tale that tells of how a certain Donald MacGregor was waylaid while returning one autumn evening to his croft in the Pass of Balmaha. Donald had been visiting some old cronies, who lived by the Gareloch. Their generosity did not end at giving him as much whisky as he could carry away inwardly: it went the length of presenting him with a full keg on his departure. Fearful was Donald lest, on his way back to Balmaha, he should meet anyone who would insist on being 'treated,' or who possibly might wrest from him his precious keg. So, stealthily he crept through the Lennox, keeping as far as possible from the beaten track to Balmaha. In course of time he arrived in a small glen near Balloch. There he sat down to take a nip or two and fell asleep. He was not long in the land of dreams when singing and dancing and the scurrying of little feet rudely awakened him to the grim reality that he had fallen asleep in a faery den. Before him stood a giant tree, into the base of which led a doorway thronged with little men and little women, who were attired in blue-bell tunics and green, broad-rimmed hats. In a trice a score of them surrounded him, and proceeded to share out the content of his keg. When the keg had been drained to the lees, the Little Folk tripped back through the doorway; and the magic tree vanished. In a state of dire confusion, Donald arose and fled to the Endrick as quickly as mere legs could bear him. Over that river he leapt in a manner never before nor since witnessed. But it was not until some day afterwards that, at a ceilidh round his own fireside in the Pass of Balmaha, he came to his senses, and recounted to his family the strange way in which he had been deprived of his keg of whisky. *MacGregor*

The Faery Dyers

In the valley between Ben Ime and Ben Vane, the tributary of the Inveruglas Water, known as Allt Coire Grogain, receives a number of trickling burns. Near the head of this valley is Lag Uaine, Green Hollow, with a faery pool in it. Upon a time the faeries of the Lennox had a dying factory by the side of this pool in the Green Hollow. Far removed from the interferences of men, they were able to keep to themselves the secret processes whereby they dyed such articles as were sent to them from time to time.

Came a day, however, when the folks of Loch Lomondside, and indeed of Loch Fyneside too, became inquisitive about the manner in which the Inveruglas faeries conducted their business in the Green Hollow. The incessant interruptions of prying neighbours sorely had tried the patience of the faeries; and they eventually began to feel that the Green Hollow was losing the seclusion that in pristine years had been so conducive to good dyeing. Many attempts to take them by surprise, while in the act of dyeing, had proved abortive. But one day a faery from his outpost on Ben Ime reported the advance on the Green Hollow of a number of men from the direction of Loch Fyne, moving up from Butterbridge, in Glen Kinglas.

Time to conceal their apparatus there was none. So, after hurried deliberations, they agreed to abandon finally their good work, and to teem their dye-stuffs with their secrets into the pool. And this explains how, to this day, the waters of this pool in the Green Hollow among the mountains have such a wonderful green colour. *MacGregor*

The Good People's Music

'As sure as you are sitting down I heard the pipes there in that wood (pointing to a wood on the north-west slope of the Hill [of Tara], and west of the banquet hall). I heard the music another time on a hot summer evening at the Rath of Ringlestown, in a field where all the grass had been burned off; and I often heard it in the wood of Tara. Whenever the Good People play, you hear their music all through the field as plain as can be; and it is the grandest kind of music. It may last half the night, but once day comes, it ends.' John Graham in Evans Wentz, *The Fairy-Faith in Celtic Countries*

The Fairy Tribes

'There is said to be a whole tribe of little red men living in Glen Odder, between Ringlestown and Tara; and on long evenings in

June they have been heard. There are other breeds or castes of fairies; and it seems to me, when I recall our ancient traditions, that some of these fairies are of the Fir Bolgs, some of the Tuatha De Danann, and some of the Milesians. All of them have been seen serenading round the western slope of Tara, dressed in ancient Irish costumes. Unlike the little red men, these fairy races are warlike and given to making invasions. Long processions of them have been seen going round the King's Chair (an earthwork on which the Kings of Tara are said to have been crowned); and they then would appear like soldiers of ancient Ireland in review.' John Boylin in *Evans Wentz*

Fairy Control Over Crops

'Fairies are believed to control crops and their ripening. A field of turnips may promise well, and its owner will count on so many tons to the acre, but if when the crop is gathered it is found to be far short of the estimate, the explanation is that the fairies have extracted so much substance from it. The same thing is the case with corn.' An Irish priest in *Evans Wentz*

Dr. Hyde and the Leprechaun

One day while I was privileged to be at Ratra, Dr. Hyde [Douglas Hyde, a Celtic scholar] invited me to walk with him in the country. After we had visited an old fort which belongs to the Good People, and had noticed some other of their haunts in that part of Queen Meave's realm, we entered a straw-thatched cottage on the roadside and found the good house-wife and her fine-looking daughter both at home. In response to Dr. Hyde's inquiries, the mother stated that one day, in her girlhood, near a hedge from which she was gathering wild berries, she saw a leprechaun in a hole under a stone. - 'He wasn't much larger than a doll, and he was most perfectly formed, with a little mouth and eyes.' Nothing was told about the little fellow having a money-bag, although the woman said people told her afterwards that she would have been rich if she had only had sense enough to catch him when she had so good a chance. *Evans Wentz*

Another Leprechaun

In going from East Ireland to Galway, during the summer of 1908, I passed through the country near Mullingar, where there was great excitement over a leprechaun which had been appearing to school-children and to many of the country-folk. I talked with some of the people as I walked through part of County Meath about this leprechaun, and most of them were certain that there could be such a creature showing itself; and I noticed, too, that they were all quite anxious to have a chance at the money-bag, if they could only see the little fellow with it. I told one good-natured old Irishman at Ballywillan – where I stopped over night – as we sat round his peat fire and pot of boiling potatoes, that the leprechaun was reported as captured by the police in Mullingar. 'Now that couldn't be, at all,' he said instantly, 'for everybody knows the leprechaun is a spirit and can't be caught by any blessed policeman, though it is likely one might get his gold if they got him cornered so he had no chance to run away. But the minute you wink or take your eyes off the little devil, sure enough he is gone.' *Evans Wentz*

The Stolen Bride

About the year 1670 there was a fine young fellow living at a place called Querin, in the County Clare. He was brave and strong and rich, for he had his own land and his own house, and not one to lord it over him. He was called the Kern of Querin. And many a time he would go out alone to shoot the wild fowl at night along the lonely strand and sometimes cross over northward to the broad east strand, about two miles away, to find the wild geese.

One cold frosty November Eve he was watching for them, crouched down behind the ruins of an old hut, when a loud splashing noise attracted his attention. 'It is the wild geese,' he thought, and raising his gun waited in deathlike silence the approach of his victims. But presently he saw a dark mass moving along the edge of the strand. And he knew there were no wild geese near him. So he watched and waited till the black mass came closer, and then he distinctly perceived four stout men carrying a bier on their shoulders, on which lay a corpse covered with a white cloth. For a few moments they laid it down, apparently to rest themselves, and the Kern instantly fired; on which the four men ran away shrieking, and the corpse was left alone on the bier. Kern of Querin immediately sprang to the place, and lifting the cloth from the face of the corpse, beheld by the freezing starlight, the form of a beautiful young girl, apparently not dead but in a deep sleep. Gently he passed his hand over her face and raised her up, when she opened her eyes and looked around with wild wonder but spake never a word, though he tried to soothe and encourage her. Then, thinking it was dangerous for them to remain in that place, he raised her from the bier, and taking her hand led her away to his own house. They arrived safely, but in silence. And for twelve months did she remain with the Kern, never tasting food or speaking word for all that time.

When the next November Eve came round, he resolved to visit the east strand again, and watch from the same place, in the hope of meeting with some adventure that might throw light on the history of the beautiful girl. His way lay beside the old ruined fort called Lios-na-fallainge (the Fort of the Mantle), and as he passed, the sound of music and mirth fell on his ear. He stopped to catch the words of the voices, and had not waited long when he heard a man say in a low whisper:

'Where shall we go to-night to carry off a bride?'

And a second voice answered:

'Wherever we go I hope better luck will be ours than we had this day twelvemonths.'

'Yes,' said a third; 'on that night we carried off a rich prize, the fair daughter of O'Connor; but that clown, the Kern of Querin, broke our spell and took her from us. Yet little pleasure has he had of his bride, for she has neither eaten nor drank nor uttered a word since she entered his house.'

'And so she will remain,' said a fourth, 'until he makes her eat off her father's table-cloth, which covered her as she lay on the bier, and which is now thrown up over the top of her bed.'

On hearing all this the Kern rushed home, and without waiting even for the morning, entered the young girl's room, took down the table-cloth, spread it on the table, laid meat and drink thereon, and led her to it.

'Drink,' he said, 'that speech may come to you.' And she drank, and ate of the food, and then speech came. And she told the Kern her story, how she was to have been married to a young lord of her own country, and the wedding guests had all assembled, when she felt herself suddenly ill and swooned away, and never knew more of what had happened to her until the Kern had passed his hand over her face, by which she recovered consciousness, but could neither eat nor speak, for a spell was on her and she was helpless. Then the Kern prepared a chariot, and carried home the young girl to her father, who was like to die for joy when he beheld her. And the Kern grew mightily in O'Connor's favour, so that at last he gave him his fair young daughter to wife; and the wedded pair lived together happily for many long years after, and no evil befell them, but good followed all the work of their hands.

This story of Kern of Querin still lingers in the faithful, vivid Irish memory, and is often told by the peasants of Clare when they gather round the fire on the awful festival of Samhain, or November Eve, when the dead walk, and the spirits of earth and air have power over mortals, whether for good or evil. Lady Wilde, *Ancient Legends, Mystic Charms, and Superstitions of Ireland*

A Legend of Innis Sark

A young man lay down to sleep one Friday evening in summer under a hay-rick and the fairies must have carried him off as he slept, because when he woke he found himself in a great hall, where a number of little men were at work - some spinning, some making shoes, some making spears and arrow-heads out of fish-bones and elf-stones; but all busy laughing and singing with much glee and merriment, while the little pipers played the merriest tunes.

Then an old man who sat in the corner came over, and looking very angry, told him he must not sit there idle; there were friends coming to dinner, and he must go down and help in the kitchen. So he drove the poor young fellow before him down into a great vaulted place, where a huge fire was burning, and a large pot was set over it.

'Now,' said the old man, 'prepare the dinner. There is the old hag we are going to eat.'

And true enough, to his horror, on looking around, there was an old woman hung up by the arms, and an old man skinning her.

'Now make haste and let the water boil,' said the old man, 'don't you see the pot on the fire, and I am nearly ready for you to begin. The company will soon be here, and there is no time to lose, for this old hag will take a good while to boil. Cut her up into little bits, and throw her into the pot.'

However, the young fellow was so frightened that he fell down on the floor speechless, and could neither move hand nor foot.

'Get up, you fool,' said another old man, who seemed to be the head over all; and he laughed at him. 'Do your work and never mind; this does not hurt her a bit. When she was there above in the world she was a wicked miser, hard to the world, and cruel and bitter in her words and works; so now we have her here, and her soul will never rest in peace, because we shall cut up the body in little bits, and the soul will not be able to find it, but wander about in the dark to all eternity without a body.'

Then the young man knew no more till he found himself in a beautiful hall, where a banquet was laid out; but, in place of the old hag, the table was covered with fruit, and chickens, and young turkeys, and butter, and cakes fresh from the oven, and crystal cups of bright red wine.

'Now sit down and eat,' said the prince, who sat at the top on a throne, with a red sash round his waist, and a gold band on his head. 'Sit down with this pleasant company and eat with us; you are welcome.'

And there were many beautiful ladies seated round, and grand noblemen, with red caps and sashes; and they all smiled at him and bade him eat.

'No,' said the young man, 'I cannot eat with you, for I see no priest here to bless the food. Let me go in peace.'

'Not at least till you taste our wine,' said the prince with a friendly smile.

And one of the beautiful ladies rose up and filled a crystal cup with the bright red wine, and gave it him. And when he saw it, the sight of it tempted him, and he could not help himself, but drank it all off without stopping; for it seemed to him the most delicious draught he ever had in his whole life.

But no sooner had he laid down the glass, than a noise like thunder shook the building, and all the lights went out; and he found himself alone in the dark night lying under the very same hay-rick where he had cast himself down to sleep, tired after his work. So he made his way home at last; but the taste of the fairy wine burned in his veins, and a fever was on him night and day for another draught; and he did no good, but pined away, seeking the fairy mansion, though he never found it any more. And so he died in his youth, a warning to all who eat the fairy food, or drink of the fairy wine; for never more will they know peace or content, or be fit for their work, as in the days before the fairy spell was on them, which brings doom and death to all who fall under the fatal enchantment of its unholy power. *Wilde*

Fairy Music

The evil influence of the fairy glance does not kill, but it throws the object into a death-like trance, in which the real body is carried off to some fairy mansion, while a log of wood, or some ugly, deformed creature is left in its place, clothed with the shadow of the stolen form. Young women remarkable for beauty, young men, and handsome children, are the chief victims of the fairy stroke. The girls are wedded to fairy chiefs, and the young men to fairy queens and if the mortal children do not turn out well they are sent back, and others carried off in their place. It is sometimes possible, by the spells of a powerful fairy-man, to bring back a living being from Fairy-land. But they are never quite the same after. They have always a spirit-look, especially if they have listened to the fairy music. For the fairy music is soft, and low, and plaintive, with a fatal charm for mortal ears.

One day a gentleman entered a cabin in the County Clare, and saw a young girl about twenty seated by the fire, chanting a melancholy song, without settled words or music. On inquiry he was told that she had once heard the fairy harp, and those who hear it lose all memory of love or hate, and forget all things, and never more have any other sound in their ears save the soft music of the fairy harp, and when the spell is broken, they die.

It is remarkable that the Irish national airs - plaintive, beautiful, and unutterably pathetic - should so perfectly express the spirit of the *Céol-Sidhe* (the fairy music), as it haunts the fancy of the people and mingles with all their traditions of the spirit world. There is a beautiful phrase in one of the ancient manuscripts descriptive of the wonderful power of Irish music over the sensitive human organization: 'Wounded men were soothed when they heard it, and slept; and women in travail forgot their pains.'

There are legends concerning the subtle charm of the fairy music and dance, when the mortal under their influence seems to move through the air with 'the naked, fleshless feet of the spirit,' and is lulled by the ecstasy of the cadence into forgetfulness of all things, and sometimes into the sleep of death. *Wilde*

Fairy Justice – The Red-haired Man

The 'Red-haired Man,' although he is considered very unlucky in actual life, yet generally acts in the fairy world as the benevolent *deus ex machina*, that saves and helps and rescues the unhappy mortal, who himself is quite helpless under the fairy spells.

There was a man in Shark Island who used to cross over to Boffin to buy tobacco, but when the weather was too rough for the boat his ill-temper was as bad as the weather, and he used to beat his wife, and fling all the things about, so that no one could stand before him.

One day a man came to him.

'What will you give me if I go over to Boffin,' said he, 'and bring you the tobacco?'

'I will give you nothing,' said the other. 'Whatever way you go I can go also.'

'Then come with me to the shore,' said the first man, 'and I'll show you how to get across; but as only one can go, you must go alone.'

And as they went down to the sea they saw a great company of horsemen and ladies galloping along, with music and laughter.

'Spring up now on a horse and you will get across,' said the first man.

So the other sprang up as he was told, and in an instant they all jumped right across the sea and landed at Boffin. Then he ran to buy the tobacco and was back again in a minute, and found all the same company by the sea-shore.

He sprang again upon a horse and they all jumped right into the sea, but suddenly stopped midway between the two islands, where there was a great rock, and beyond this could not force the horses to move. Then there was great disquietude amongst them, and they called a council.

'There is a mortal amongst us,' they said. 'Let us drown him.' And they carried the man up to the top of the rock and cast him down; and when he rose to the surface again they caught him by the hair, and cried 'Drown him! Drown him! We have the power over life and death and he must be drowned.'

And they were going to cast him down a second time, when a red-haired man pleaded for him, and carried him off with a strong hand safe to shore.

'Now,' said he, 'you are safe, but mind, the spirits are watching you, and if ever again you beat your poor good wife, and knock about the things at home just to torment her out of her life, you will die upon that rock as sure as fate.' And he vanished.

So from that time forth the man was as meek as a mouse, for he was afraid; and whenever he went by the rock in his boat he always stopped a minute, and said a little prayer for his wife with a 'God bless her.' And this kept away the evil, and they both lived together happily ever after to a great old age. *Wilde*

The Fairy Dance

The following story is from the Irish, as told by a native of one of the Western Isles, where the primitive superstitions have still all the freshness of young life.

One evening late in November, which is the month when spirits have most power over all things, as the prettiest girl in all the island was going to the well for water, her foot slipped and she fell. It was an unlucky omen, and when she got up and looked round it seemed to her as if she were in a strange place, and all around her was changed as if by enchantment. But at some distance she saw a great crowd gathered round a blazing fire, and she was drawn slowly on towards them, till at last she stood in the very midst of the people; but they kept silence, looking fixedly at her; and she was afraid, and tried to turn and leave them, but she could not.

Then a beautiful youth, like a prince, with a red sash, and a golden band on his long yellow hair, came up and asked her to dance.

'It is a foolish thing of you, sir, to ask me to dance,' she said, 'when there is no music.'

Then he lifted his hand and made a sign to the people, and instantly the sweetest music sounded near her and around her, and the young man took her hand, and they danced and danced till the moon and the stars went down, but she seemed like one floating on the air, and she forgot everything in the world except the dancing, and the sweet low music, and her beautiful partner. At last the dancing ceased, and her partner thanked her, and invited her to supper with the company.

Then she saw an opening in the ground, and a flight of steps, and the young man, who seemed to be the king amongst them all, led her down, followed by the whole company. At the end of the stairs they came upon a large hall, all bright and beautiful with gold and silver and lights; and the table was covered with everything good to eat, and wine was poured out in golden cups for them to drink.

When she sat down they all pressed her to eat the food and to drink the wine; and as she was weary after the dancing, she took the golden cup the prince handed to her, and raised it to her lips to drink. Just then, a man passed closed to her, and whispered 'Eat no food, and drink no wine, or you will never reach your home again.' So she laid down the cup, and refused to drink. On this they were angry, and a great noise arose, and a fierce, dark man stood up, and said 'Whoever comes to us must drink with us.' And he seized her arm, and held the wine to her lips, so that she almost died of fright. But at that moment a red-haired man came up, and he took her by the hand and led her out.

'You are safe for this time,' he said.

'Take this herb, and hold it in your hand till you reach home, and no one can harm you.'

And he gave her a branch of a plant called the *Aithair-Luss* (the ground ivy). This she took, and fled away along the sward in the dark night; but all the time she heard footsteps behind her in pursuit.

At last she reached home and barred the door, and went to bed, when a great clamour arose outside, and voices were heard crying to her.

'The power we had over you is gone through the magic of the herb; but wait - when you dance again to the music on the hill, you will stay with us for evermore, and none shall hinder.'

However, she kept the magic branch safely, and the fairies never troubled her more; but it was long and long before the sound of the fairy music left her ears which she had danced to that November night on the hillside with her fairy lover. *Wilde*

Ethna the Bride – Finvarra

The fairies, as we know, are greatly attracted by the beauty of mortal women, and Finvarra the king employs his numerous sprites to find out and carry off when possible the prettiest girls and brides in the country. These are spirited away by enchantment to his fairy palace at Knockma in Tuam, where they remain under a fairy spell, forgetting all about the earthly life and soothed to passive enjoyment, as in a sweet dream, by the soft low melody of the fairy music, which has the power to lull the hearer into a trance of ecstasy.

There was once a great lord in that part of the country who had a beautiful wife called Ethna, the loveliest bride in all the land. And her husband was so proud of her that day after day he had festivals in her honour; and from morning to night his castle was filled with lords and ladies, and nothing but music and dancing and feasting and hunting and pleasure was thought of.

One evening while the feast was merriest, and Ethna floated through the dance in her robe of silver gossamer clasped with jewels, more bright and beautiful than the stars in heaven, she suddenly let go the hand of her partner and sank to the floor in a faint. They carried her to her room where she lay long quite insensible; but towards morning she woke up and declared that she had passed the night in a beautiful palace, and was so happy that she longed to sleep again and go there in her dreams.

And they watched by her all the day, but when the shades of evening fell dark on the castle, low music was heard at her window, and Ethna again fell into a deep trance from which nothing could rouse her. Then her old nurse was set to watch her; but the woman grew weary in the silence and fell asleep, and never awoke till the sun had risen. And when she looked towards the bed, she saw to her horror that the young bride had disappeared.

The whole household was roused up at once, and search made everywhere, but no trace of her could be found in all the castle, nor in the gardens, nor in the park. Her husband sent messengers in every direction, but to no purpose - no one had seen her; no sign of her could be found, living or dead. Then the young lord mounted his swiftest steed and galloped right off to Knockma, to question Finvarra, the fairy king, if he could give any tidings of the bride, or direct him where to search for her; for he and Finvarra were friends, and many a good keg of Spanish wine had been left outside the window of the castle at night for the fairies to carry away, by order of the young lord. But he little dreamed now that Finvarra himself was the traitor; so he galloped on like mad till he reached Knockma, the hill of the fairies. And as he stopped to rest his horse by the fairy rath, he heard voices in the air above him, and one said:

'Right glad is Finvarra now, for he has the beautiful bride in his palace at last; and never more will she see her husband's face.'

'Yet,' answered another, 'if he dig down through the hill to the centre of the earth, he would find his bride; but the work is hard and the way is difficult, and Finvarra has more power than any mortal man.'

'That is yet to be seen,' exclaimed the young lord.

'Neither fairy, nor devil, nor Finvarra himself, shall stand between me and my fair young wife,' and on the instant he sent word by his servants to gather together all the workmen and labourers of the country round with their spades and pickaxes, to dig through the hill till they came to the fairy palace. And the workmen came, a great crowd of them, and they dug through the hill all that day till a great deep trench was made down to the very centre. Then at sunset they left off for the night; but next morning when they assembled again to continue their work, behold, all the clay was put back again into the trench, and the hill looked as if never a spade had touched it - for so Finvarra had ordered; and he was powerful over earth and air and sea. But the young lord had a brave heart, and he made the men go on with the work; and the trench was dug again, wide and deep into the centre of the hill. And this went on for three days, but always with the same result, for the clay was put back again each night and the hill looked the same as before, and they were no nearer to the fairy palace. Then the young lord was ready to die for rage and grief, but suddenly he heard a voice near him like a whisper in the air, and the words it said were these:

'Sprinkle the earth you have dug up with salt, and your work will be safe.'

On this new life came into his heart, and he sent word through all the country, to gather salt from the people; and the clay was sprinkled with it that night, when the men had left off their work at the hill. Next morning they all rose up early in great anxiety to see what had happened, and there to their great joy was the trench all safe, just as they had left it, and all the earth, round it was untouched. Then the young lord knew he had power over Finvarra, and he bade the men work on with a good heart, for they would soon reach the fairy palace now in the centre of the hill. So by the next day a great glen was cut right through deep down to the middle of the earth, and they could hear the fairy music if they put their ear close to the ground and voices were heard round them in the air.

'See now,' said one, 'Finvarra is sad, for if one of those mortal men strike a blow on the fairy palace with their spades, it will crumble to dust, and fade away like the mist.'

'Then let Finvarra give up the bride,' said another, 'and we shall be safe.'

On which the voice of Finvarra himself was heard, clear like the note of a silver bugle through the hill:

'Stop your work,' he said. 'Oh, men of earth, lay down your spades, and at sunset the bride shall be given back to her husband. I, Finvarra, have spoken.'

Then the young lord bade them stop the work, and lay down their spades till the sun went down. And at sunset he mounted his great chestnut steed and rode to the head of the glen, and watched and waited; and just as the red light flushed all the sky, he saw his wife coming along the path in her robe of silver gossamer, more beautiful than ever; and he sprang from the saddle and lifted her up before him, and rode away like the storm wind back to the castle. And there they laid Ethna on her bed; but she closed her eyes and spoke no word. So day after day passed, and still she never spoke or smiled, but seemed like one in a trance. And great sorrow fell upon every one, for they feared she had eaten of the fairy food, and that the enchantment would never be broken. So her husband was very miserable. But one evening as he was riding home late, he heard voices in the air, and one of them said:

'It is now a year and a day since the young lord brought home his beautiful wife from Finvarra; but what good is she to him? She is speechless and like one dead; for her spirit is with the fairies though her form is there beside him.' Then another voice answered:

'And so she will remain unless the spell is broken. He must unloose the girdle from her waist that is fastened with an enchanted pin, and burn the girdle with fire, and throw the ashes before the door, and bury the enchanted pin in the earth; then will her spirit come back from fairy-land, and she will once more speak and have true life.'

Hearing this the young lord at once set spurs to his horse, and on reaching the castle hastened to the room where Ethna lay on her couch silent and beautiful like a waxen figure. Then, being determined to test the truth of the spirit voices, he untied the girdle, and after much difficulty extracted the enchanted pin from the folds. But still Ethna spoke no word; then he took the girdle and burned it with fire, and strewed the ashes before the door, and he buried the enchanted pin in a deep hole in the earth, under a fairy thorn, that no hand might disturb the spot. After which he returned to his young wife, who smiled as she looked at him, and held forth her hand. Great was his joy to see the soul coming back to the beautiful form, and he raised her up and kissed her; and speech and memory came back to her at that moment, and all her former life, just as if it had never been broken or interrupted; but the year that her spirit had passed in Fairy-land seemed to her but as a dream of the night, from which she had just awoke. After this Finvarra made no further efforts to carry her off; but the deep cut in the hill remains to this day, and is called 'The Fairy's Glen.' So no one can doubt the truth of the story as here narrated. *Wilde*

The Fairies of Tullamore

An old woman living near Tullamore Park, Co. Down, described vividly how, going out to look after her goat and its young kid, she had heard loud screams and seen wild-looking figures with scanty clothing whose hair stood up like the mane of a horse. She spoke with much respect of the fairies as the gentry, said they formerly inhabited hills in Tullamore Park, and that care was taken not to destroy their thorn-bushes. She related the following story: As a friend of hers was sitting alone one night, a small old woman, dressed in a white cap and apron, came in and borrowed a bowl of meal. The debt was repaid, and the meal brought by the fairy put in the barrel. The woman kept the matter secret, and was surprised to find her barrel did not need replenishing. At last her husband asked if her store of meal was not coming to an end; she replied that she would show him she had sufficient, and lifted the cover of the barrel. To her astonishment it was almost empty; no doubt, had she kept her secret, she would have had an unlimited supply of meal. Andrews, *Ulster Folklore*

The Fairy Spinning-Wheel

A woman was spinning one evening when three fairies came into the house, each bringing a spinning-wheel. They said they would help her with her work, and one of them asked for a drink of water. The woman went to the well to fetch it. When there she was warned, apparently by a friendly fairy, that the others had come only to mock and harm her. Acting on the advice of this friend, the woman, as soon as she had given water to the three, turned again to the open door, and stood looking intently towards a fort. They asked what she was gazing at, and the reply was: 'At the blaze on the fort.' No sooner had she uttered these words than the three fairies rushed out with such haste that one of them left her spinning-wheel behind, which, according to the story, is now to be seen in Dublin Castle. The woman then shut her door, and put a pin in the keyhole, thus effectually preventing the return of her visitors. *Andrews*

The Herd-Boy and the Fairy Mother

I have heard several similar stories, and have not found that any evil consequences were supposed to follow from partaking of food brought by the fairies. Men have been carried off by them, have heard their beautiful music, seen them dancing, or witnessed a fairy battle without bringing any misfortune on themselves. On the other hand, according to a story I heard at Buncrana, Co. Donegal, a little herd-boy paid dearly for having entered one of their dwellings. As he was climbing among the rocks, he saw a cleft, and creeping through it came to where a fairy woman was spinning with her 'weans,' or children, around her. His sister missed him, and after searching for a time, she too, came to the cleft, and looking down saw her brother, and called to him to come out. He came, but was never able to speak again. *Andrews*

Fairy Property

To cut down a fairy thorn or to injure the house of a fairy is regarded as certain to bring misfortune.

An old woman living at Maghera, related how her great-grandmother had received a visit from a small old woman, who forbade the building of a certain turf-stack, saying that evil would befall anyone who injured the chimneys of her house. The warning was disregarded, the turfstack built, and before long four cows died. *Andrews*

The Old Woman with the Green Cloak

An elderly woman in Co. Antrim told me that when a child she one evening saw 'a little old woman with a green cloak coming over the burn.' She helped her to cross, and afterwards took her to the cottage, where her mother received the stranger kindly, told her she was sorry she could not give her a bed in the house, but that she might sleep in one of the outhouses. The children made Grannie as comfortable as they could, and in the morning went out early to see how she was. They found her up and ready to leave. The child who had first met her said she would again help her across the burn. 'But wait,' she added, 'until I get my bonnet.' She ran into the house, but before she came out the old woman had disappeared. When the mother heard of this she said: 'God bless you, child! Don't mind Grannie; she is very well able to take care of herself.' And so it was believed that Grannie was a fairy. *Andrews*

The Fairy Child

There have been from time immemorial at Hawick, during the two or three last weeks of the year, markets once a week, for the disposal of sheep for slaughter, at which the greater number of people, both in the middle and poorer classes of life, have been accustomed to provide themselves with their marts. A poor man from Jedburgh who was on his way to Hawick for the purpose of attending one of these markets, as he was passing over that side of Rubislaw which is nearest the Teviot, was suddenly alarmed by a frightful and unaccountable noise. The sound, as he supposed, proceeded from an immense number of female voices, but no objects whence it could come were visible. Amidst howling and wailing were mixed shouts of mirth and jollity, but he could gather nothing articulate except the following words:

'O there's a bairn born, but there's naething to pit on 't.'

The occasion of this elfish concert, it seemed, was the birth of a fairy child, at which the fairies, with the exception of two or three who were discomposed at having nothing to cover the little innocent with, were enjoying themselves with that joviality usually characteristic of such an event. The astonished rustic finding himself amongst a host of invisible beings, in a wild moorland place, and far from any human assistance, should assistance be required, full of the greatest consternation, immediately on hearing this expression again and again vociferated, stripped off his plaid, and threw it on the ground. It was instantly snatched up by an invisible hand, and the wailings immediately ceased, but the shouts of mirth were continued with increased vigour.

Being of opinion that what he had done had satisfied his invisible friends, he lost no time in making off, and proceeded on his road to Hawick, musing on his singular adventure. He purchased a sheep, which turned out a remarkably good bargain, and returned to Jedburgh. He had no cause to regret his generosity in bestowing his plaid on the fairies, for every day afterwards his wealth multiplied, and he continued till the day of his death a rich and prosperous man. Gibbings, *Folk-Lore and Legends: Scotland*

The Loan of Meal

About the beginning of harvest, there having been a want of meal for shearer's bread in the farmhouse of Bedrule, a small quantity of barley (being all that was yet ripe) was cut down, and converted into meal. Mrs. Buckham, the farmer's wife, rose early in the morning to bake the bread, and, while she was engaged in baking, a little woman in green costume came in, and, with much politeness, asked for a loan of a capful of meal. Mrs. Buckham thought it prudent to comply with her request. In a short time afterwards the woman in green returned with an equal quantity of meal, which Mrs. Buckham put into the meal-ark. This meal had such a lasting quality, that from it alone the gudewife of Bedrule baked as much bread as served her own family and the reapers throughout the harvest, and when harvest was over it was not exhausted. *Gibbings*

A Banshee Story

The Caointeach was a Banshee. She followed the Clan MacKay and other clans in the Rhinns of Islay. When a death was going to happen in one of these clans, she would come to the sick man's house with a green shawl about her shoulders, and give his family warning by raising a sad wail outside the door. As soon as the sick man's friends heard her voice, they lost all hope of his getting better. They had heard the Caointeach lamenting, and that was proof enough to them that his end was at hand.

The Caointeach has ceased to give warning to the people of the Rhinns. She was last heard at a house in that district many years ago.

A sick man was then on his death-bed, and his friends attending him. It was winter, and the night was wet and cold, with rain and wind. She stood at the windward door of the house; and there she raised a low, melancholy wail. The family heard her mourning; and one of them so pitied her that he went out at the leeward door, and left her an old plaid on a seat at the side of the door. He then returned within, and cried to her:

'Come to the sheltered side, poor woman; and cover yourself with a piece of my plaid.'

In an instant the lamenting ceased; and from that time to this the Caointeach has not been seen or heard in the Rhinns.
MacDougall

The Black Lad MacCrimmon and the Banshee

It appears that the fairies were excellent musicians, and that their choice of all musical instruments was the bag-pipes. Often did the wayfarer hear its sound coming from the Fairy Knoll, which happened to be in his path, and often did he feel its sweet music tempting him to walk in, and lift his foot in the dance with the fairies.

This art which they possessed they are said to have taught to some men for whom they took a liking, and who are still remembered in tradition. Amongst these was the Black Lad MacCrimmon.

Up to the Black Lad's time, the MacCrimmons were no better than other good pipers in the Highlands. He was the first of them who rose above all the rest in fame, and who was commonly called 'The King of Pipers.'

He was the youngest of three sons, and the least thought of by his father. When his father would take down from the back of the crooked stick the great bag-pipes, which he called the Black Gate, and he himself would play the first tune on it, he would hand it to his eldest son, and when his eldest son had done with it, he would hand it to the second son; but when the second son had done with it, the Black Lad would not get the honour of blowing so much as one blast into the bag. He was also kept down by the rest, and left to do every piece of work that was more slavish than another.

On a certain day, his father and his two brothers went to the fair, and left him alone at home. After they had gone, he got hold of the chanter, and began to play upon it. And in the midst of the playing, who should come upon him but the Banshee from the Castle.

'Thou art busy discoursing music, Lad,' said she.

He answered that he was.

'Which wouldst thou prefer, skill without success, or success without skill?' said she then.

He answered that he would rather have skill without success. She pulled hair from her head, and asked him to put it round the reed of the chanter. When he had done that, she said to him:

'Place now thy fingers on the holes of the chanter, and I will lay my fingers on thy fingers.'

As soon as that was done, she said:

'When I shall lift my finger, lift thou the finger which happens to be under it. Think now of any tune thou pleasest, and play it with me in the way I have told thee.'

He did so, and played the tune skilfully. When he had finished the tune, she said:

'Now thou art the King of Pipers. Thine equal was not before thee, and thine equal shall not be after thee.'

She then bade him good day, and departed.

As soon as she had gone, he took down the Black Gate and began playing on it. There was not a tune he could think of which he did not try and which he could not play with ease. Before he ceased his father and brothers had returned from the fair. And when they approached the house, they heard the music, and stood to listen.

'Whoever is playing, it is on the Black Gate,' said the father to his sons.

They went on, but the music ceased before they reached the house.

They went in, but none of them let on that they had heard the music till night came. Then the old man took down the great bag-pipes, and after he himself and his two eldest sons had played tune about, he asked the Black Lad to take his own spell of it.

'Is it I?' said he, 'I am not worthy of that honour. It is enough for me to be a slave to you all.'

'Take the bag-pipes, and thou shalt no longer be asked to do slavish work,' said his father.

He took the pipes at last, and struck up the finest music any one in the house had ever heard. 'The music has left us,' said the father to the other sons. 'None of us will come in the wake of the Black Lad.' He spake truly, for the like of the Black Lad never lived, either in his own time, or since. *MacDougall*

2 GLAISTIG

Donald MacIan's First Adventure with the Glastig of Ben Breck

Donald MacIan was cow-herd with the tenantry of Achantore in Lochaber. When summer came round, he went with the cattle on the farm to the summer pastures of Ben Breck, on the north side of the Blackwater.

One day, as he sat on the meadow at the foot of the Ben, and the cattle were lying round about him, he heard a small voice far away; and immediately he looked in the direction whence it came. What did he behold, coming with great speed and making straight for the place where he was sitting, but a Glastig? Without a moment's delay, he drew out of her way and tried to hide himself in a bush of bog-myrtle. But if he did, it was not without being observed by her. She turned the way he went, and, in the twinkling of an eye, was standing by his side. She then began to leap forward and back again over his body, clapping her hands, and repeating the following words:

Am faic sibh am bramachan roidein
'Na laighe am measg nam bó?
Bhuaileadh e buille eadar dà bhuille
Is buille eadar dà dhòrn,
'San lòn eadar dà dhoire
'San doire eadar dà lòn?

'Do you see the wee colt of the sweet gale
Lying in the midst of the kine?
A stroke he would strike between two strokes,
And a stroke between two blows,
In the meadow between two groves,
In the grove between two meadows.'

When she grew tired of that work, she went away with a light, playful spring, singing the following lilt:

Is mire mi na'm fior-eun mór
Is mire mi na'm fior-eun òg,
Is mire mi na laogh dà bhó,
Is mire mi na meann an crò.

'Friskier am I than the great eagle,
Friskier am I than the young eagle,
Friskier am I than the calf of two cows,
Friskier am I than a kid in a fold;'

And going with such speed that poor Donald, the herd, who was half dead with fear, could not see her feet moving on the ground. She kept on at this rate, stooping and pulling with her teeth tufts of grass from the earth, until she went out of sight.
MacDougall

Donald MacIan's Second Adventure with the Glastig of Ben Breck

The same Donald MacIan went with the Achantore cattle to Ben Breck another summer. He reached the sheiling bothy at Ruighe-na-cloiche, beside Ciaran Water, about evening. On the way he gathered an armful of fuel and took it with him to the bothy. He set the fuel in order on the hearth-stone, seized the fire implements, and, after striking fire, began to kindle the fuel.

In the midst of this work he thought he heard a strange cry, far off at first, and soon after much nearer. At length he heard the same voice outside the house saying:

'Heigh! Ho! Hal!

Has this man over the way left yet?'

Scarcely had he turned his eye the way the voice came, when the door opened, and a Glastig stood before him in the opening. She cried aloud: 'Donald MacIan, I was on the Uralich when you put the first spark in the tinder, and in the Woodpecker's Corrie when the wisp took fire; and here I am now as the fuel is beginning to kindle.' 'Thou hast walked well, poor creature,' said Donald MacIan.

She now attempted to come in; but if she did, Dergan, the herd's dog, attacked her. 'Stop Dergan, Donald MacIan,' said she. Donald MacIan pretended to stop the dog, but that he could not. 'Tie thy dog, Donald MacIan,' said she then. 'I have nothing to tie him with,' answered the herd. She pulled a grey hair out of her head, and handed it to him, saying: 'Tie him with that.' The herd pretended to do what he was told, but put his own garter on the dog instead of the Glastig's hair.

As soon as she thought that the dog was tied, she flew at the herd; but if she did, Dergan flew at her. She then cried: 'Tighten and choke, hair! Tighten and choke, hair!' But the herd threw the hair in the fire, and it crackled and crackled until it flew out through the roof of the bothy. No sooner was that over than the dog got loose, and fastened on the Glastig. She cried at the pitch of her voice: 'Take the dog off me, Donald MacIan, and I will give thee no more trouble.' The herd did as she told him, and then she said to him: 'Go to Ben Breck early to-morrow, Donald MacIan, and thou wilt find the White Hind which thou hast been hunting for many a day, but which thou hast not yet caught.' After she had said this, she made for the door.

Early nexy day the herd took with him his bow and arrows and went to Ben Breck. When he reached the Ben, he saw the Glastig coming to meet him, with a herd of deer before her, and the White Hind at their head. He took aim at the Hind, and let go the arrow. But before the arrow left the bend of the yew, he heard the

Glastig crying, in a spiteful tone: 'Stick in the stomach, arrow. Stick in the stomach.' The arrow did stick in the White Hind's stomach, and Donald MacIan got it home with him, as was promised him. *MacDougall*

The Croon of the Glastig of Ben Breck

This is the Croon which the Glastig of Ben Breck used to sing to her hinds while she was driving them before her on the mountain side:

Cailleach Beinne Bric, horó!
Bric horó! Bric horó!
Cailleach Beinne Bric, horó!
Cailleach mhór an fhuarain àird
Cha leiginn mo bhuidheann fhiadh
Bhuidheann fhiadh, bhuidheann fhiadh,
Cha leiginn mo bhuidheann fhiadh
A dh' iarraidh shlige duibh' a 'n tràigh.
Gu'm b' annsa leò biolair fhuar,
Biolair fhuar, biolair fhuar,
Gu'm b' annsa leò biolair fhuar,
A bhiodh an cois an fhuarain àird.

Lady of Ben Breck, Horo![5]
Breck, horo! Breck, horo!
Lady of Ben Breck, horo!
Lady of the fountain high.
I ne'er would let my troop of deer,
Troop of deer, troop of deer;

[5] *Cailleach* more properly means 'old woman, hag' rather than 'lady', but the translation of 'lady' is fitting for her role as guardian of the mountain.

I ne'er would let my troop of deer
A-gathering shellfish to the tide.
Better liked they cooling cress,
Cooling cress, cooling cress;
Better liked they cooling cress,
That grows beside the fountain high. *MacDougall*

The Onich Brothers and the Glastig of Ben Breck

There once lived in Onich two brothers who were exceedingly fond of hunting and fishing. In summer time and harvest, they used to go to the Black Mount, and while they stayed there, they took shelter in the shieling-bothy of The Dun Valley of the Moss at the heel of Ben Breck.

Here the Glastig used to visit them, until she and they grew as well acquainted with each other as though they had been always neighbours. But the hunters had no pleasure in her company, for she was so troublesome that they were obliged to be always on their guard against her.

One of the brothers, named Gillesbick, was patient with her; but the other, whose name was Ronald, was not. Gillesbick was displeased with his brother for his conduct, because he was afraid of provoking the nasty hag to be revenged on them. So, when his brother would turn against her with his dirk, and she would cry: 'Stop Ronald, Lasbick,' Lasbick would angrily say: 'Won't you let the poor creature alone?' Then she would turn on himself, for she could not keep a moment quiet, and ask of him for snuff, with the intention of seizing his hand when reaching it to her, and of carrying him off with her. But he would put the snuff on the point of the dirk, and present it to her that way. Then she would bend her arm, and turn the point of her elbow towards him, and say: 'Put it on this, Lasbick.' But Lasbick knew that the object of this request was to get a hold, first of the handle of the dirk, and then of himself. This put him on his guard against her, so that he kept her off with the point of the dirk.

On a certain day she, by her teasing, put Ronald in such a passion that he suffered the terrier to attack her. Gillesbick cried to him to stop the dog and let her alone. Ronald turned a deaf ear to this; and instead of stopping the terrier he incited the grey hound also to attack her. This greatly kindled her wrath. She gave him one stern look askance, and before going off said: 'Perhaps I'll pay thee back for this yet, my lad.'

After she had gone, Gillesbick said to his brother: 'Ill hast thou done. I fear that virago will do us harm yet.' But his brother replied that there was no fear of them as long as they would have the grey hound and the terrier.

Next night at bed time they heard a small voice, at first as if it were far away, and shortly afterwards as if it were nearer them. The voice was coming nearer and nearer, and that with great speed. At length Gillesbick cried to Ronald: 'It is the Glastig! Take hold of thy dirk quickly, and be ready for her when she arrives.' Ronald drew his dirk; and the grey hound, with an angry look, sprang up at his side. He then urged the dog and the terrier on, and they at once made their way out with a rush to meet the Glastig.

The two brothers stayed in the bothy listening to hear what should happen. They had not been long waiting until they heard the loud barking which began outside. This noise continued long about the door, but gradually it went further away from the house. At last when night began to turn to day, the fight ceased and the dogs returned to the bothy.

The big dog came first with only a tuft of hair here and there on his body; and shortly after him came the terrier as bare as a newly plucked hen. *MacDougall*

The Hunter and the Glastig of Ben Breck

A hunter was one day returning from Ben Breck, and when he arrived at the foot of the mountain, he thought he heard a sound like the cracking of two stones striking together, or the rattling of a stag's horns when he rubs them against a rock. He held on his way, until he came in sight of a large stone that lay beside the path, and then he saw, crouching at the foot of the stone, the semblance of a woman, with a green shawl about her shoulders, and in her hands a pair of deer-shanks, which she kept striking against one another without ceasing. Though he understood that she was the Glastig, he made bold enough to say to her: 'What are you doing there, poor woman?' But the only reply he got was: 'Since the wood was burnt, since the wood was burnt,' and she kept repeating this refrain as long as he was within hearing distance of her. *MacDougall*

An Iona Glaistig

In the shieling days of Iona when, during the summer months, the inhabitants of the east end and of the west end of that Island were wont to pasture their cows alternately for fourteen days on the common grazing at a spot known as Staonnaig, a Glaistig dwelt in a hollow rock near at hand. For this Glaistig the Iona women at milking-time each evening poured a little milk on what is still pointed out as the Glaistig's Stone.

The story goes that on one occasion this Glaistig came to the house of an old woman in Iona, seeking shelter from a heavy downpour. The old woman, whose name was Livinstone, prepared a meal for her, and bade her dry her wet clothes by the peat-fire. Before the glowing peats stood the Glaistig, extending her clothes to the warmth. Suddenly they caught fire. This so annoyed her that she rendered it impossible thereafter for any woman of the name of Livinstone to kindle or re-fuel a fire on Iona while a meal stood ready for consumption. *MacGregor*

'A Grey Stone Overgrown With Lichen'

Not unlike the activities of the Brownie [the Scotch name for the household spirit] were the activities of the Glaistig that took up her residence at a farmhouse in Glen Duror of Appin, in Argyll. This Glaistig interested herself chiefly in the Glen Duror cattle; and she regarded it as her especial duty to prevent the calves from suckling their mothers during the night.

This Glaistig did not follow the tenants of the farm from place to place. The farmhouse in Glen Duror was her permanent residence. Incoming tenants were told of her by those outgoing, and were handed over to her charge – certainly so far as the milk-giving stock was concerned. This Glaistig, it is said, was alive as late as 1870, and may still be alive for all we know! Those who claimed to having seen her described her facial expression as resembling 'a grey stone overgrown with lichen.'

Every evening for several generations a small quantity of milk was poured into a stone for this Glaistig; and this stone is still referred to in Duror of Appin as the *Clach na Glaistig*, the Glaistig's Stone. But there came to the farmhouse in course of time a new tenant who omitted to supply this offering, with the result that next morning the calves were found among the cows, and there was no milk in their udders for the porridge.

When a servant lassie at this farm was asked whether she had any fear of giving displeasure to the Glaistig, she ridiculed the idea. The result was that, when she was proceeding to a stream nearby to obtain a pailful of water in the dark, she received a sharp slap on the cheek that gave a twist to her neck. Howbeit, when on the same errand the following evening, she received

another slap on the other cheek that corrected the twist!
MacGregor

3 *EACH UISGE*, KELPIE

The Water-Horse of Poll nan Craobhan

In bygone days, Poll nan Craobhan, a pool on the river Spey, in Cromdale, was haunted by a water-horse which was the terror of the surrounding country. At certain seasons he was to be seen feeding with the cattle on the bank of the river; and then he seemed to be the most beautiful horse that man ever beheld. His coat was a black and glossy as the raven's wing. On his head was a glittering bridle, and on his back a saddle with stirrups of silver. But when any man, bolder than his fellows, approached too near him, one glance of the horse's fiery eye sent a thrill of terror through him that rooted him to the earth, so that he could not move hand or foot. If, in his fear, the man then forgot to cross himself, the black horse of the most beautiful shape would draw nearer and nearer him, and the fierce glance of his eye would change to the mild look of the deer. When he would come up to the man, he would fawn on him by rubbing his shining head against his breast.

Soon the man's fear would vanish, and he would spring into the saddle; and then, quick as an arrow from the bow, the black horse would plunge into the Poll nan Craobhan. The man was to be seen no more, and the black horse was not to be seen for a year and a day.

Near the river Spey lived a man named Little John. Little John usually spent a great part of the year in the Yellow Moss making peats, and on that account he was known over the length and breadth of the parish as Little John of the Yellow Moss. Though Little John, as his name indicates, was very small in person, he was as bold and fearless as one of the very *Féinn* [the Fianna, the ancient warrior band of Scotland and Ireland]. His thoughts all day and his dreams by night were of the water horse in Poll nan Craobhan; and many were the fruitless plans he formed for the destruction of the horse.

At long last, he thought he would go and consult the black wife of Alnaic; and he was not long in leaving Cromdale Hill behind him. When he arrived at the hut of the black wife, he knocked at the door, and the answer came out at once: 'Come in, Little John of the Yellow Moss; it is I who am aware what you want; and who knows but you and I may yet put a tether on the black horse of Poll nan Craobhan.'

When John had got enough sowens and sweet milk, the black wife took her divining stone, and looked into it for a long time. At last she lifted up her head, and said: 'Now, Little John, I know well that you are no coward, and that you will subdue the water horse of Poll nan Craobhan.' 'I do not know about that,' said Little John. 'Keep up you heart, and there is no fear of you! But this is what you must do: The horse will be feeding on the meadow on Beltane-eve. When the sun begins to descend from his highest point in the sky, you will kill the speckled ox. You will then put the skin about yourself, and go on your hands and feet, like an ox. Before the setting of the sun let someone drive yourself and the cows to the side of Poll nan Craobhan. As soon as the sun sets, the black horse will come up out of the water, and begin feeding with the cattle. As you will look like an ox, the horse will be thrown off his guard. But if you feel or show the least fear, your wife will look for your return in vain. Draw nearer and nearer the river at your leisure, until you get between the horse and the water; and then it will be your own fault if you get not the better of him. The bridle has neither bit nor chin-strap; and, therefore, when you get near enough, you will make a spring at the bridle, and pull it off. The black horse is then under your control, and will do whatever you wish, so long as you keep the bridle from him. Be careful of the bridle, or it will be the worse for you. Now, Little John, go your way.'

Little John went home, and waited till the day before Beltane-eve came round. As soon as the sun had crossed his highest point in the sky, he killed the speckled ox. His wife put the skin upon him in such a clever way that the very cows mistook him for the ox that had been killed. Before sunset she drove the cows to the bank of the river, and he followed as best he could. When the sun went down, the black horse came slowly up out of the pool, and began feeding among the cattle. Said Little John to himself: 'Now, son of my own father, be not afraid,' and pretending to be nibbling the grass as he went, he at last got between the horse and the water. Then with a great spring he got hold of the glittering bridle, pulled it off the horse, and caught him by the forelock.

'Ha, ha! my lad, I have you now,' said he.

The horse answered: 'You have me now, indeed, Little John of the Yellow Moss; but if you will show me the same kindness as you show to your other animals, I will serve you faithfully day and night, until you give me back my own bridle and saddle by the hand of a maiden; and then I will trouble the country no more.'

'We will see about that,' said Little John.

Great was the terror of Little John's wife when she saw the awful beast being led to the stable; but Little John assured her that the water-horse of Poll nan Craobhan would yet make their fortune.

Little John hid the bridle and the saddle in a secret corner above the kitchen bed. No man was so proud as he; for no horse in the course of the Spey could be compared with his beautiful black horse. No road was too rough for him to tread, no load too heavy to carry, no fodder too coarse to eat. With his great sled-cart Little John could now empty the Yellow Moss of peats quicker than the men of the Clachan could build them into stacks.

He was getting rich, and many came from far and near to buy the black horse; but they were left to return home without him.

Things went on in this way with Little John for some years, until one day he and his wife went to a fair at the Clachan of Cromdale, and left their daughter Sheena Vane to look after the horse. Sheena Vane used to feed the black horse with her own hand, and ride him to water; but on this black, evil day she happened to light upon the bridle and saddle, where they lay concealed.

She thought to herself that now was her chance of having a good long ride on the black horse's back; and away she went with the bridle and saddle to the stable. When the horse saw his own furniture, he neighed at it with great delight. In a short time he was in harness; but no sooner was Sheena Vane seated on the saddle than away he went with the swiftness of the wind, not to Poll nan Craobhan, but to a Lochan near the Clachan of Cromdale. As they were going through Achroisk they were met by Little John and his wife, and the black horse cried out in passing: 'I have now got my bridle and saddle from the hands of a maiden, and I will trouble no man anymore.'

The horse and the maiden were seen to plunge headlong into the deepest part of the Lochan, where many believed it had no bottom. That was the last that was seen of Sheena Vane and the water-horse of Poll nan Craobhan, but not the last that was heard of Sheena, as will presently be seen.

It was observed that the part of the Lochan in which the black horse disappeared with Sheena Vane never froze over, however thick the ice might be on the surrounding water. In the cold winter nights, when the wind blew strong, and swept the snow in blinding clouds from Cromdale Hill, an eerie, piteous cry of: 'I am cold, I am cold,' was heard above the noise of the storm, coming from the Lochan and sending a cold chill through the hearts of those that heard it. Year after year the same mournful cry was heard, until a smith from Glen Braon came and settled in the Clachan. This smith had been taught by the black wife of Alnaic how to speak to ghosts; and when he first heard the piteous cry, he said that he would soon see what the ghost was wanting.

He went out to the Lochan, and used the words he had learned from the black wife of Alnaic; and the ghost told him that it could not find rest until the priest had said seven masses for the soul of Sheena Vane. The mass was said, and the eerie cry of: 'I am cold, I am cold,' was not heard thereafter. The Lochan is called to this day Bog-an-Loirein; and the place where Little John of the Yellow Moss lived, Dalchapple (Horsefield). *MacDougall*

The White Horse of Spey

Among the folks of Spey-side there was an ancient belief that the loss of life by drowning in that river was due to the alluring machinations of the White Horse of Spey, a creature described by them as a beautiful beast to the sight, but in reality a kelpie of ill-doing. Seldom during good weather was the White Horse seen, or was there any evidence of its evil existence. But on boisterous nights, when thunders pealed among the Cairngorms and the Hills of Cromdale, his whinnying was often heard, and his form almost as frequently seen. And it was his custom in circumstance of storm, they say, to accost benighted pedestrians and assure them of safe escort to their destination. By the side of the footsore wanderer he would walk, until the former became so overcome with fatigue as to accept gladly the offer of being conveyed astraddle for the remainder of his journey. Once a-mount the White Horse of Spey, the rider's fate was sure, for the fearsome creature then galloped off at break-neck pace, and plunged into the deep pools of the Spey, carrying with him the rider who, by some power of magic, remained fixed immovably to its back.

Tradition in Spey-side has it that the White Horse claimed innumerable victims in this way; and of the exultant song sung by the White Horse, in his death-dash, the following fragment has been handed down to us:

'And ride weel, Davie,
And by this night at ten o'clock
Ye'll be in Pot Cravie.'

In her charming book, The Secret of Spey, Wendy Wood gives another fragment of the White Horse's song, which she picked up locally:

'Ride you;
Ride me.
Kelpie,
Creavie!'

Yet another version of the kelpie's song is given by a Cairney contributor to the official journal of the Banff Field Club in 1884. 'I remember, when children,' writes this contributor, 'we used to be told that the water-kelpie would sing to the poor, deluded ones he managed to entice away:'

'Sit weel, Janety, or ride weel, Davie,
For this time the morn ye'll be in Pot Cravie.' *MacGregor*

The Kelpie's Stane

By the Bridge of Luib, on the River Don, is a boulder known to the natives as the Kelpie's Stane. It happened that a man summoned to the death-bed of a relative came to this crossing-place just after torrential floods had carried away the bridge. When he was on the point of abandoning all hope of reaching the opposite bank, a tall man appeared from nowhere, and volunteered to carry him across. The distracted homecomer accepted the assistance proffered. But, when he and his carrier reached mid-river, the latter reverted to the form of the river kelpie, and endeavoured to drag him down to the river's bed. The victim managed to escape. As he scrambled to the bank, the infuriated kelpie hurled after him the huge boulder that to this day goes by the name of the Kelpie's Stane. *MacGregor*

The Doomed Rider

'The Conan is as bonny a river as we hae in a' the north country. There's mony a sweet sunny spot on its banks, an' mony a time an' aft hae I waded through its shallows, whan a boy, to set my little scautling-line for the trouts an' the eels, or to gather the big pearl-mussels that lie sae thick in the fords. But its bonny wooded banks are places for enjoying the day in – no for passing the nicht. I kenna how it is; it's nane o' your wild streams that wander desolate through a desert country, like the Aven, or that come rushing down in foam and thunder, ower broken rocks, like the Foyers, or that wallow in darkness, deep, deep in the bowels o' the earth, like the fearfu' Auldgraunt; an' yet no ane o' these rivers has mair or frightfuller stories connected wi' it than the Conan. Ane can hardly saunter ower half-a-mile in its course, frae where it leaves Coutin till where it enters the sea, without passing ower the scene o' some frightful aul legend o' the kelpie or the waterwraith. And ane o' the most frightful looking o' these places is to be found among the woods of Conan House. Ye enter a swampy meadow that waves wi' flags an' rushes like a corn-field in harvest, an' see a hillock covered wi' willows rising like an island in the midst. There are thick mirkwoods on ilka side; the river, dark an' awesome, an' whirling round an' round in mossy eddies, sweeps away behind it; an' there is an auld burying-ground, wi' the broken ruins o' an auld Papist kirk, on the tap. Ane can see amang the rougher stanes the rose-wrought mullions of an arched window, an' the trough that ance held the holy water. About twa hunder years ago – a wee mair maybe, or a wee less, for ane canna be very sure o' the date o' thae old stories – the building was entire; an' a spot near it, whar the wood now grows thickest, was laid out in a corn-field. The marks o' the furrows may still be seen amang the trees.

A party o' Highlanders were busily engaged, ae day in harvest, in cutting down the corn o' that field; an' just aboot noon, when the sun shone brightest an' they were busiest in the work, they heard a voice frae the river exclaim:

'The hour but not the man has come.'

Sure enough, on looking round, there was the kelpie stan'in' in what they ca' a fause ford, just fornent the auld kirk. There is a deep black pool baith aboon an' below, but i' the ford there's a bonny ripple, that shows, as ane might think, but little depth o' water; an' just i' the middle o' that, in a place where a horse might swim, stood the kelpie. An' it again repeated its words: 'The hour but not the man has come,' an' then flashing through the water like a drake, it disappeared in the lower pool. When the folk stood wondering what the creature might mean, they saw a man on horseback come spurring down the hill in hot haste, making straight for the fause ford. They could then understand her words at ance; an' four o' the stoutest o' them sprang oot frae amang the corn to warn him o' his danger, an' keep him back. An' sae they tauld him what they had seen an' heard, an' urged him either to turn back an' tak' anither road, or stay for an hour or sae where he was. But he just wadna hear them, for he was baith unbelieving an' in haste, an' wauld hae taen the ford for a' they could say, hadna the Highlanders, determined on saving him whether he would or no, gathered round him an' pulled him frae his horse, an' then, to mak' sure o' him, locked him up in the auld kirk. Weel, when the hour had gone by – the fatal hour o' the kelpie – they flung open the door, an' cried to him that he might noo gang on his journey. Ah! but there was nae answer, though; an' sae they cried a second time, an' there was nae answer still; an' then they went in, an' found him lying stiff an' cauld on the floor, wi' his face buried in the water o' the very stone trough that we may still see amang the ruins. His hour had come, an' he had fallen in a fit, as 'would seem, head-foremost amang the water o' the trough, where he had been smothered, - an' sae ye see, the prophecy o' the kelpie availed naething.' *Gibbings*

4 URUISG

The Urisk of Sgurra-a-Chaorainn

An Urisk once lived in a steep rock at the foot of Sgurr-a-Chaorainn in Lochaber. This Urisk was, it appears, very troublesome to the herd of Blar-a-Chaorainn, when he happened to go the way of Sgurr. Not an evening he passed it but the Urisk put his head out of a hole in the face of the rock and bawled after him: 'Carl, son of carl, son of carl. There you have of carls three: a carl are you, and a carl is your father, and your son will be a carl, and his son will be a carl, and you all will be carls, like it or not.'

When this herd left Blar-a-Chaorainn, there came in his place another whom his acquaintances called Donald Mór. Donald was but a short time on the farm, until he was as much annoyed by the Urisk as the herd that had left. Not an evening did he return from the hill past the rock but the Urisk bawled after him:

'Donald Mór, I do not like you.'

This salutation was far from being pleasing to honest Donald, but he kept his opinion to himself as long as he could. At length his patience was so completely worn out by the Urisk's continual jeering that he could not contain himself any longer.

One evening, when returning, cold and hungry, from the hill, and the Urisk bawling after him as usual:

'Donal Mór, I do not like you,'

Donald turned on his heel in wrath, and bawled as loud as the Urisk himself: 'That is but the return you owe me.' The Urisk ceased his jeering; and from that time to this his voice has not been heard by any other person. *MacDougall*

The Urisk of Eas Buidhe

In Glen Mallie, in Lochaber, there is an eerie ravine called Eas Buidhe. In this ravine it was said that the Urisks took refuge; and near it were the summer pasture bothies of some of the farmers in the Glen.

One of the Urisks,

Uruisg an Eas'-Bhuidhe
'Na shuidhe 'n Gleann-Màilidh.

'The Urisk of Eas Buidhe,
Sitting in Glen Maillie,'

was very troublesome to one of the dairymaids staying in the bothies near the ravine. Not a day passed but he came to the bothy where she lived; and he spent the time sitting at the fire, asking questions, and obstructing her in her work. She grew tired of him, but she knew not how to rout him without turning the wrath of the other Urisks against her. At last her patience with him was so completely worn out that she resolved to get rid of him, happen what might.

One day as he was crouching about the fire as usual, he asked, among his questions, what her name was. She replied that it was:

'Myself and Myself.'

'That is a curious name,' said he.

'Never mind, that is what I am called.'

A pot full of whey hung over the fire, and when she went to take it off, he was in her way, as usual. This so provoked her that she intentionally allowed a wave of the boiling whey to fall on his feet, and scald him. He sprang up quickly from his seat, and ran out, howling and crying that he was burnt. As soon as the other Urisks heard this, they ran up from the ravine to meet him, and asked who burnt him. He answered that it was 'Myself and Myself.'

'Oh, if you have burnt yourself, it cannot be helped; but if anyone else had done it, we would have burnt him and all that is in the bothies along with him.' *MacDougall*

Big Alastair and the Urisk

Big Alastair was as good and as keen a rod-fisher as there was in his native place. As soon as he would see the appearance of a good shower coming, he would instantly throw his rod over his shoulder, and he would hie away at a trotting pace to the river.

On a warm summer evening, with a good drizzling rain falling accompanied with mist, he, as his custom was, betook himself to the river; and after getting his rod in order, he therewith cast out the tackle. As soon as the hook touched the water, the fish began to take better than he had ever seen them take before. He was hauling the trout in so thickly, one after another, that he had no time to wait to put them on either withy or string. He just threw them on the green grass on the bank of the river, with the intention of returning for them when the fishing was over. His attention was so much on his work that night came upon him without his observing it. He then gave a look behind him, and whom did he see, fishing at his side, but a great Urisk, who was taking in trout for trout with him, and throwing them with his own catch of fish upon the grass. There was no help for it, and no use in saying a syllable. But he and his companion kept on at the fishing until the best part of the night was overpast. Then the Urisk cried:

'It is time to stop, Big Alastair, and divide the fish.'

'No! No!' said Big Alastair, 'it is not at all time, while the fish are taking so well.'

Without saying more the Urisk returned sulkily to the fishing. A good while after that, he cried again:

'Stop now, Big Alastair, and let us divide the fish.'

'Have patience a little longer,' said Alastair, 'considering that I never before saw the fish in such a taking humour.'

The Urisk did as he was asked, but it was not willingly; for the day was approaching, and another fishing to accomplish before it would arrive. So, in a short while, he cried the third time to

Alastair to stop. Alastair knew, from the tone of the monster's voice that there was no use whatever in asking a longer delay.

Whereupon he turned towards him and said:

'Whether wilt thou gather the fish, or divide them?'

The Urisk answered:

'I shall gather them, and do thou divide them.'

'I do not know how to divide them,' said Alastair.

'Pooh! that is not difficult. A spratlum down, and a spratlum up; a spratlum there, and a spratlum here; and the last big spratlum for me.'

This division pleased Alastair very indifferently, for he understood that he himself was the big spratlum which the Urisk wished to have as his share of the fish before the day should come. But what was he to do to disappoint the nasty fellow? The day was approaching, and if he could keep the work unfinished until it came, he would be safe.

He began to divide the fish, but to all appearance he was in no hurry to finish that task. When the fish would not slip out of his hands, he would make a mistake in the counting, or some other mishap would occur to delay him. The Urisk was losing his patience, and no mischance would befall Alastair which did not inflame his wrath.

He would shake his head and shoulders, stamp on the ground with his feet, and in a voice half angry, half plaintive, cry out: 'Won't thou take care, Big Alastair? Won't thou take care, Big Alastair?'

But Alastair would suffer his remonstrance to go in at one ear and out the other.

At length the red cock awoke, and relieved him from the straight he was in. He crowed on a knoll above the river, and straightway the Urisk went out of sight.

Alastair took with him the fish, and returned home. But from that day to the day of his death he did not go to fish trout on the river after nightfall. *MacDougall*

5 MERMAIDS (*MORUADH*) AND SEAL FOLK

The Seal Catcher's Adventure

There was once upon a time, a man who lived on the northern coasts, not far from Taigh Jan Crot Callow (John-o'-Groat's House), and he gained his livelihood by catching and killing fish, of all sizes and denominations. He had a particular liking to the killing of those wonderful beasts, half dog half fish, called 'Roane', or Seals, no doubt because he got a long price for their skins, which are not less curious than they are valuable. The truth is, that the most of these animals are neither dogs nor cods, but downright fairies, as this narration will show; and, indeed, it is easy for any man to convince himself of the fact by a simple examination of his tobacco-spluichdan, - for the dead skins of those beings are never the same for four and twenty hours together. Sometimes the spluichdan will erect its bristles almost perpendicularly, while, at other times, it reclines them even down; ... what dead skin, except itself, could perform such cantrips? Now, it happened one day, as this notable fisher had returned from the prosecution of his calling, that he was called upon by a man who seemed a great stranger, and who said, he had been dispatched for him by a person who wished to contract for a quantity of seal-skins, and that it was necessary for the fisher to accompany him immediately to see the person who wished to contract for the skins, as it was necessary that he should be served that evening. Happy in the prospect of making a good bargain, and never suspecting any duplicity in the stranger, he instantly complied. They both mounted a steed belonging to the stranger, and took the road with such velocity that, although the direction of the wind was towards their backs, yet the fleetness of their movement made it appear as if it had been in their faces. On reaching a stupendous precipice which overhung the sea, his guide told him, they had now reached the point of their destination. 'Where is the person you spoke of?' inquired the astonished seal-killer. 'You shall see that presently,' replied the guide. With that they immediately alighted, and, without allowing the seal-killer much time to indulge the frightful suspicions that began to pervade his mind, the stranger seized him with irresistible force, and plunged headlong with the seal-killer into the sea. After sinking down – down – nobody knows how far, they at length reached a door, which, being open, led them into a range of apartments, filled with inhabitants – not people, but seals, who could nevertheless speak and fell like human folk; and how much was the seal-killer surprised to find that he himself had been unconsciously transformed into the like image. If it were not so, he would probably have died, from the want of breath. The nature of the poor fisher's thoughts may be more easily conceived than described. Looking on the nature of the quarters into which he was landed, all hopes of escape from them appeared wholly chimerical, whilst the degree of comfort, and length of life which the barren scene promised him, were far from being flattering. The 'Roane,' who all seemed in very low spirits, appeared to feel for him, and endeavoured to soothe the distress which he evinced, by the amplest assurances of personal safety. Involved in sad meditation of his evil fate, he was quickly roused from his stupor, by his guide's producing a huge gully or joctaleg, the object of which he supposed was to put an end to all his earthly cares. Forlorn as was his situation, however, he did not wish to be killed; and, apprehending instant destruction, he fell down, and earnestly implored for mercy. The poor generous animals did not mean him any harm, however much his former conduct deserved it; and he was accordingly desired to pacify himself, and cease his cries. 'Did you ever see that knife before?' says the stranger to the fisher. The latter instantly recognising his own knife, which he had that day stuck into a seal, and with which it made its escape, acknowledged it was formerly his own, for what would be the use of denying it? 'Well,' rejoins the guide, 'the apparent seal, which made away with it, is my father, who lies dangerously ill ever since, and no means could stay his fleeting breath, without your

aid. I have been obliged to resort to the artifice I have practised to bring you hither, and I trust that my filial duty to my father will readily operate my excuse.' Having said this, he led into another apartment the trembling seal-killer, who expected every minute a return of his own favour to the father; and here he found the identical seal, with which he had the encounter in the morning, suffering most grievously from a tremendous cut in its hind-quarter. The seal-killer was then desired, with his hand, to cicatrize the wound, upon doing which, it immediately healed, and the seal arose from its bed in perfect health. Upon this, the scene changed from mourning to rejoicing – all was mirth and glee. Very different, however, were the feelings of the unfortunate seal-catcher, expecting, no doubt, to be a seal for the remainder of his life, until his late guide accosted him as follows: 'Now, Sir, you are at liberty to return to you wife and family, to whom I am about to conduct you; but it is on this express condition, to which you must bind yourself by a solemn oath, viz. that you shall never maim or kill a seal in all your lifetime hereafter.' To this condition, hard as it was, he joyfully acceded; and the oath being administered in all due form, he bade his new acquaintance most heartily and sincerely a long farewell. Taking hold of his guide, they issued from the place, and swam up – up – till they regained the surface of the sea; and, landing at said stupendous pinnacle, they found their former riding steed ready for a second canter. The guide breathed upon the fisher, and they became like men. They mounted their horse; and fleet as was their course towards the precipice or pinnacle, their return from it was doubly swift; and the honest seal-killer was laid down at his own door-cheek, where his guide made him such as present, as would have almost reconciled him to another similar expedition, and such as rendered his loss of profession, in so far as regarded the seals, a far less intolerable hardship than he had at first contemplated it.
Stewart, *The Popular Superstitions and Festive Amusements of the Highlanders of Scotland*

A Mermaid

A man had become enamoured of a mermaid whom he first espied combing her 'ling lang yellow locks' while he was wandering along the shore. He was warned by a sea god that swift death awaited him if he pursued his suit. Finally he was persuaded by threats and bribes to turn his attention back to a lass of his own race who had tarried for him inland. The lover told his adviser, though he would do as he was bidden he would not forget the halcyon days of summer he had spent, lingering by the tide with the fair lady of the sea who had entranced him. The merman, struck by the landsman's fondness for all that appertained to his watery realm, promised him that his descendants would likewise be ocean lovers. Before the earth dweller turned his steps inland to woods and fields the sea god baptised him with the splash of a wave. His race in this country grew and increased, and sure enough, the fascination for the salt water never left them. Simpson, *Folk Lore in Lowland Scotland*

The Shannon Mermaid

'Sure [said the old woman], 'twas over there beyond the corner where the river is that the mermaid was caught, and Deny Duegan described her to me, and he the oldest man in Foynes. The man that caught her was one of those who watched the weir over on the Island. They were forever seeing a woman on the point, and they knew it was the mermaid that was ever living in the river, and one day the man saw her sitting on a big stone on the point and she a-combing her fine golden hair back from the forehead of her, and combing it from the rack. And he faced round and crept up behind her when she was not knowing it, and caught her by the two shoulders of her, and brought her to his house, where his mother lived.'

'It was the beautifullest woman ever you see'd, with the golden hair and fair skin of her. Now after a time he took her as his wife, and she had three children to him, and all the time she was doing all the work a woman might do, but never a smile or a laugh out of her, except one day when he was a-doing something with the child on the floor, playing with it, and then she let the sweetest laugh out of her that ever you heard. Now the man had taken the covering from her that she had the day sitting on the rock, a sort of an oily skin, and he had been told to keep it from her and put it away by way of luck.'

'And the house was built so that the fireplace had piers like on each side of it, as in the country houses, and on the top a shelf, and 'twas on this that the man had put away the covering among the nets and sacks. For—she was going about the house doing all the work that a woman might do, but that she could never climb up on a thing, and she afeared even to stand on a chair to reach a thing as might be. But one day—it was seven years from the day he had caught her on the stone and brought her home—she was sitting by the fire with the child, and he just able to walk. He was on her knee sitting, when the man came in looking for the net, and he began to throw things about on the shelf looking for it. Well, he threw down an old sack out of the way of him, and with it sure the covering fell down, and he never seeing it, and it fell behind her so as she couldn't lay hand to it with the child on her knee; so she looked over her shoulder and saw it, and she put the child to stand with the chair, went and took the covering and out of the door with it before the man had time to get down and stop her, and down to the shore she went with a laugh as never you heard with the ringing in it, and into the sea, and she never came back again.'

'And the three children of her were reared on the island over beyond Deny Duggan's, and 'tis three ages [generations] ago now, for Deny he is the oldest man in Foynes, and when he was young he knew the children of her, and heard of her from a friend of the man that worked with him on the weir.' Colum, *A Treasury of Irish Folklore*

The Seal-Folk in Ireland

Until quite recent times, the inhabitants of Donegal and of the many islands lying off the west coast of Ireland believed the seal to be of human origin, and capable of casting its skin and assuming human form. The natives of Achill Island, for example, still speak of their seal ancestry; and the old folks of Achill strongly resent the killing of seals along the neighbouring coasts.

Authorities on Irish folk-lore tell us that the families of Coneely, O'Sullivan, O'Flaherty, and Mac-na-Mara are directly descended from the Seal-folk. To this day it is quite a common occurrence to meet in western Ireland Gaels who not only accept the tradition of the Seal-folk, but even declare that they have seen seals in the process of metamorphosis, have spoken with them at such times, and have listened to their singing. There is a tradition in the west of Ireland that in ancient times members of the Coneely family, who are regarded as being one of the earliest septs to settle in the country, were changed into seal-men and seal-women by 'art magick.' Thus it is that no Coneely can slay a seal without incurring ill-fortune and the censure of his kindred. *MacGregor*

The MacPhees of Colonsay

Belief that drowned persons sometimes assumed the form of seal-men and seal-women, and that they were able periodically to lay aside their seal-skins and assume human proportions during the night-time and return to the sea as seals at sunrise, was prevalent in Ireland, in the Western Highlands, in the Outer Hebrides, and in the Orkneys and Shetlands.

Tradition has it that the MacPhees of Colonsay, an island of the Inner Hebrides, are of the stock of a seal-woman, whose seal-skin was discovered on a rock one day, and carried off to a house near at hand by an unthinking islander. However, the owner did not rest until she recovered her seal-skin, whereupon she returned to her life in the sea.

One of the MacPhees – so it is believed in Argyll and in the Hebrides – was retained in captivity in a cavern by the shore of Colonsay by a seal-woman, who ministered to all his requirements, except to the need he always expressed for his freedom. Came a day when MacPhee, taking advantage of the seal-woman's temporary absence, effected his escape. But, on her returning to find that he had gone, the seal-woman instantly gave pursuit. MacPhee fled to the protection of his home, where he kept a dog, black of hue, and fierce – so fierce, in truth, that the Colonsay folks dreaded it, and often tried to persuade MacPhee to dispose of it. But MacPhee consistently gave them the same reply.

'The Black Dog's day is yet to come!' he always urged, this being a Gaelic equivalent of the saying, 'Every dog has its day!'

Now, the seal-woman overtook the fleeing MacPhee by the shore; and she would have captured him, had not the black dog engaged her. And the old folks of Colonsay, reciting island folk-lore at their ceilidhs round the peat-fires on winter nights, narrate that the contest between dog and seal-woman continued until the black dog killed the seal-woman, and the seal-woman killed the black dog! *MacGregor*

Clan MacCodrum of the Seals

In the Hebrides it is believed that the seals were royal attendants in the Palaces of Lochlann (Norway), in the Land of the King of Sleep, whence they came to the shores of Western and Northern Scotland and of Ireland in the capacity of secret emissaries in the service of the Kings of Lochlann.

The North Uist sept known as the Clan MacCodrum of the Seals, a sept of the historic Clan Ranald of the Isles, has been named traditionally, and for centuries, the Children of the Seals. The tradition of the Seal-folk as it existed in the Hebrides is alluded to by Sheriff Nicolson among his collection of Gaelic proverbs, where he makes mention of the *Clann Mhic-Codruim nan Ròn*, the Children of MacCodrum of the Seals. Nicolson recites the Seal-folk legend concerning the MacCodrums' having been metamorphosed into seals. But, though they altered their form, they still retained their human souls. In the Outer Hebrides generally, and in North Uist particularly, popular belief has it that the MacCodrums were seals by day, and human beings by night. And, since the MacCodrums were conscious of their seal affinity, nothing would induce them to kill or molest or injure a seal in any way.

Whereas the natives of Western Ireland refrained from interfering with seals because they looked upon them as transformed human beings, the MacCodrums of the Hebrides showed them the greatest deference, not merely because they believed them to be of human origin, but because they believed them to be of their very own flesh and blood – their very kith and kin.

Seal-folk tradition in the Western Highlands and Islands asserts that the Clan MacCodrum of the Seals derived its title from a progenitor who, when wandering by the shore of his Hebridean isle, came upon a company of seals when they were in the act of discarding their seal-coats before bathing themselves. Home with one of the coats dashed MacCodrum; and he was on the point of concealing his find above the lintel of his door when its seal-woman owner followed him in. This seal-woman MacCodrum restrained from returning to the sea. He clothed her with garments similar to those worn by ordinary human beings on his native Island of North Uist. Later he married her, and by her he had a large family. This *clann* or family became known throughout the Western Isles and even in Ireland as the Children of MacCodrum of the Seals. But one day, when MacCodrum was away from home, his seal-woman wife searched the house for her seal-skin. On finding it, she donned it once more, and immediately returned to her sea-kindred. *MacGregor*

BIBLIOGRAPHY

Andrews, E., *Ulster Folklore* (New York: E. P. Dutton & Co., 1919).

Campbell, J. G. & Black, R. (ed.), *The Gaelic Otherworld* (Edinburgh: Birlinn, 2008).

Colum, P., *A Treasury of Irish Folklore* (Crown Publishers, 1954).

Croker, T. C., *Fairy Legends and Traditions of the South of Ireland*, vols. 1-3 (London: John Murray, 1825 and 1828).

Evans Wentz, W. Y., *The Fairy-Faith in Celtic Countries* (London: Oxford University Press, 1911).

Gibbings, W. W., *Folk-Lore and Legends: Scotland* (London, 1889).

MacDougall, J. & Calder, G. (ed.), *Folk Tales and Fairy Lore in Gaelic and English* (Edinburgh: John Grant, 1910).

MacGregor, A. A., *The Peat-Fire Flame: Folk-Tales and Traditions of the Highlands & Islands* (Edinbugh: The Moray Press, 1937).

Simpson, E.-B., *Folk Lore in Lowland Scotland* (London: J. M. Dent & Co., 1908).

Stewart, W. G., *The Popular Superstitions and Festive Amusements of the Highlanders of Scotland* (Edinburgh: Archibald Constable and Company, 1823)

Wilde, *Ancient Legends, Mystic Charms, and Superstitions of Ireland* (Boston: Ticknor and Co., 1887).

Yeats, W. B., *Irish Fairy Tales* (London: T. Fisher Unwin, 1892).

www.ingramcontent.com/pod-product-compliance
Ingram Content Group UK Ltd.
Pitfield, Milton Keynes, MK11 3LW, UK
UKHW040604210726
13854UKWH00009B/2636

9 781838 344009